HF5667 .D397 1981
The auditor–client contractual relations
3 1569 00144 308 1

WITHDRAWN FROM LIBRARY

COLLIER LIBRARY
University of North Alabama
FLORENCE, ALABAMA

The Auditor-Client Contractual Relationship
An Economic Analysis

The Auditor-Client Contractual Relationship
An Economic Analysis

by
Linda Elizabeth DeAngelo

UMI RESEARCH PRESS
Ann Arbor, Michigan

Copyright © 1981, 1980
Linda Elizabeth DeAngelo
All rights reserved

Produced and distributed by
UMI Research Press
an imprint of
University Microfilms International
Ann Arbor, Michigan 48106

Library of Congress Cataloging in Publication Data

DeAngelo, Linda Elizabeth.
 The auditor-client contractual relationship.

 (Research for business decisions ; no. 43)
 Revision of thesis (Ph.D.)–University of Washington, 1980.
 Bibliography: p.
 Includes index.
 1. Auditing. I. Title. II. Series.
HF5667.D397 1981   657'.45   81-12923
ISBN 0-8357-1241-9   AACR2

To Harry

Contents

Acknowledgments

1 Introduction *1*

2 Corporate Contracting Relationships and the Demand for Audit Services as a Monitoring Device *7*
   2.1 Owner-Management Contracting
   2.2 Intra-Owner Contracting
   2.3 Who Bears the Cost of Audit Services?

3 On the Nature of Audit Services *17*
   3.1 Audit Services and Free Rider Problems
   3.2 The Observability of Audit Output and the Brand Name Mechanism

4 Auditor Independence and the Intertemporal Pricing of Audit Services *33*
   4.1 The Economic Benefits of Auditor Independence
   4.2 The Existence of Specialized Assets Creates Future Economic Interest
   4.3 Current Regulatory Interest
   4.4 A Two-Period Model of Audit Pricing
   4.5 Testable Implications and Current Regulation

5 Specialized Assets, Number of Clients, and Length of the Auditor-Client Relationship *51*
   5.1 Explicit and Implicit Contracting for the Exchange of Audit Services
   5.2 Auditor Size and the Collateral Bond Effect of Specialized Assets
   5.3 Choice of Length of the Auditor-Client Relationship
   5.4 Testable Implications and Extant Evidence

6 Economies in Audit Technology and Auditor Industry Specialization   77
   6.1 Industry-Level Learning in Auditing
   6.2 A Formal Model of Auditor Industry Specialization
   6.3 Extant Evidence on Auditor Industry Specialization

7 Conclusions   95

Appendix A: Requirements for Membership in the AICPA SEC Practice and Private Companies Practice Sections   99

Appendix B: Multiperiod, Infinite Horizon Audit Pricing Model   103

Appendix C: Summary of Regulation Governing Changes of Auditor   107

Appendix D: The Use of Engagement Letters to Formalize Auditor-Client Relationships   109

Notes   113

Bibliography   123

Index   127

Acknowledgments

I wish to express my sincere appreciation to Professors William L. Felix, Jr., Yoram Barzel, Nancy L. Jacob, Eric Noreen, David L. Ragozin, Edward M. Rice, and Gary L. Sundem. Professors Felix, Barzel, Noreen, and Rice gave unselfishly of their time in reading several versions of this study. In particular, I have especially benefited from the helpful guidance provided by Bill Felix, and from lengthy discussions with and insightful comments from Ed Rice.

I would also like to express my gratitude to my parents, Ralph and Winifred Buckley, without whose regard for education I would not have valued it so highly myself. Dorothy Blair also deserves special thanks for providing early encouragement. In addition, Joan Shearer's professional attitude and excellent typing skills have been a great help on the many drafts of this work.

Last, but by no means least, for his intellectual stimulation, constant encouragement, friendship, and for the academic example he sets, I wish to thank my husband, Harry DeAngelo.

1

Introduction

> Because most of the formal economic models of competition, exchange, and equilibrium have ignored ignorance and lack of costless full and perfect information, many institutions of our economic system, institutions that are productive in creating knowledge more cheaply than otherwise, have been erroneously treated as parasitic appendages.
>
> —Armen Alchian in "Why Money?"

Recent advances in the theory of the firm[1] have attempted to deal with the issue of how individuals contract among themselves when

(1) There are potential benefits to be gained from cooperation, e.g., team production, specialization, etc., and

(2) Contracting among individuals is costly due to the imperfect ability of the parties to foresee and specify *ex ante* all possible future contingencies. In addition, information asymmetries (either *ex ante* or *ex post*) may provide individuals with the opportunity to benefit from opportunistic behavior.[2]

The existence of conditions (1) and (2) leads to a demand for (costly) monitoring arrangements which enable those individuals who possess the property rights to productive opportunities to capture potential benefits associated with cooperation. Audited financial statements are one possible monitoring technology. The continued existence of this arrangement for over 600 years (see Watts and Zimmerman [July 1979]) suggests that it is an important monitoring technology which economizes on the costs of contracting.

The purpose of this research is to contribute to a positive theory of auditing[3] by modeling the structure of auditor-client contractual relationships. In particular, we seek to explain the equilibrium pricing of audit services and the length of the auditor-client relationship in response to differences in the regulatory environment and (both firm and industry level) learning-by-doing advantages. The theory developed generates several testable implications about audit fees, auditor concentration, and the frequency with which client firms change auditors.

The importance of developing a positive theory of auditing is that an understanding of "what is" and how the current system reacts to exogenous changes is desirable as input into auditing policy decisions. As Watts [1977] states it, "the development of prescriptions which are likely to achieve their objectives requires an underlying theory which explains observed phenomena: which predicts the effects of particular prescriptions."

Extant auditing research has not studied the interaction between the pricing of audit services and issues of auditor independence in a rigorous fashion. And yet, this relationship is an important concern of both the auditing profession and the Securities and Exchange Commission. In particular, both these parties are concerned about the alleged practice of quoting a fixed fee or limited per unit time fee on a first time audit which is below total cost in that period, i.e., the practice of "low-balling." For example, the Commission on Auditors' Responsibilities (the Cohen Commission) was charged in 1974 by the American Institute of Certified Public Accountants to "develop conclusions and recommendations regarding the appropriate responsibilities of independent auditors." The Commission Report, issued in 1978, contends that

> An ethics ruling of the AICPA indicates that when the preceding year's audit fee remains unpaid, independence is impaired. This prohibition is based on the belief that such a receivable from the client gives the auditor an interest in the financial success of the client and might influence his independence in carrying out the examination.
> We believe that accepting an audit engagement with the expectation of offsetting early losses or lower revenues with fees to be charged in future audits creates the same condition and represents the same threat to independence. (p. 121).

The Securities and Exchange Commission, partly in response to the Cohen Commission Report, issued Securities Exchange Act Release No. 33-5869 in September, 1977. In this release, the SEC proposed that proxy statements disclose the fees paid to independent auditors for the past two years and the services provided by the auditors for the most recent year. Firms would also be required to disclose in proxy statements the existence of fixed fee arrangements or any other "ceiling" on audit fees, whether explicitly or implicitly agreed to by the parties. According to Release No. 33-5869,

> The Commission is also concerned about the possible effect on the auditor's independence and objectivity of any understanding or agreement limiting the auditor's fee to an absolute amount. Accordingly, the proposed rule would require disclosure of any such agreement.

The SEC solicited comments on Release No. 33-5869 and the final rule, ASR-250, which became effective for proxy statements subsequent to September 30, 1978 reads,

> Describe any existing direct or indirect understanding or agreement that places a limit on current or future years' audit fees, including fee arrangements that provide fixed limits on fees that are not subject to reconsideration if unexpected issues involving accounting or auditing are encountered.

The theoretical link between "low-balling" and auditor independence was not explored prior to the implementation of regulation designed to curtail the practice. One of the major contributions of this study is to formulate a theory which makes this link. Specifically, the theory presented in Chapter 4 predicts that "low-balling" is a competitive response to the existence of client-specific learning-by-doing advantages, positive transactions costs of changing auditors, and competition in the market for audit services.[4] The implications of the theory for auditing policy and extant regulation are also explored in Chapter 4.

The Chapter 4 model is a one-auditor, one-client analysis. In Chapter 5, we formulate a model of the auditor's choice of the number of clients in his "portfolio." Within this framework we analyze the auditor's incentives to lower audit quality by attesting falsely to the financial statements of a given client. We show that auditor opportunism of this type is constrained by the threat of withdrawal of future business from the auditor's other clients. Intuitively, while the existence of future economic interest in a given client impairs auditor independence with respect to that client, the existence of future economic interest in other clients serves as a collateral bond to guarantee audit quality.[5]

Another important contribution of this study is to provide a theory that potentially explains the frequency with which firms change auditors. Several studies[4] have presented empirical evidence on the frequency of auditor changes. None of these studies has supplied a rigorous formalization of the incentives which drive a client's change of auditors. In Chapter 5, we formulate a theory which predicts that the firm's decision to change auditors is a tradeoff between

(1) the cost savings of retaining the incumbent auditor for future audits, and

(2) the negative impact on client firm value of maintaining a relationship with an auditor who possesses "future economic interest" in the client.

Future economic interest arises because the existence of learning-by-doing advantages and positive transactions costs of changing auditors provides an incumbent auditor with a comparative cost advantage over competitors in future periods. This cost advantage enables the incumbent auditor to charge higher (than total costs) future fees, thus creating the "future economic interest" which the accounting profession and the SEC view as impairing auditor independence. The effects of extant regulation requiring disclosure of the circumstances surrounding a change of auditors are also discussed in Chapter 5.

An important assumption of the analysis in the first five chapters of this book is that auditor knowledge can be partitioned into two mutually exclusive and exhaustive subsets:

(1) general knowledge applicable in auditing all potential clients, and

(2) specialized knowledge applicable to auditing one particular client.

In actuality, there are likely to be economies in audit technology within different groups of clients because of operational and organizational similarities within an industry, the existence of industry-specific auditing or accounting standards, or regulation which affects a group of client firms in a like manner. For simplicity, we label this effect industry-level learning-by-doing advantages, while recognizing that the common element among the group is the audit technology, rather than client industry affiliation per se. Thus, in addition to general and firm-specific knowledge, industry knowledge is likely to be an important factor in the exchange of audit services.

The effect of industry-level learning-by-doing advantages on the portfolio of clients chosen by auditors is the subject of Chapter 6. The formal model developed in that chapter predicts that an increase in industry learning advantages provides an incentive for auditors to increase industry specialization only if it lowers their costs relative to their competitors' costs. If it raises their costs relative to their competitors' costs, auditors will have the incentive to reduce the number of industry clients. Under competitive conditions, the critical variable which drives the result is shown to be the assumed relationship between client-specific and industry-level learning-by-doing advantages.

An important contribution of the industry model is that it provides a rigorous formalization of the incentives for auditor specialization by industry. Several empirical studies[7] have documented industry specialization by auditing firms. The importance of developing such a theory to explain this observed phenomenon is emphasized by Zeff and Fossum [1967]:

> The data presented in this paper barely scratch the surface of a potentially fascinating area of study, namely, how public accounting firms grow, develop, and acquire personalities. What factors, planned or fortuitous, cause firms to specialize in (or avoid) particular industries? . . . it would seem that the most instructive and informative chapters in the history of the U.S. public accounting profession are yet to be written. (p. 306)

The theory developed in Chapter 6 represents an attempt to shed light on some of these questions.

This study is organized as follows: the first three chapters explore the demand for, and nature of audit services. Formal models of audit pricing, client composition, and the length of the auditor-client relationship are presented in Chapters 4, 5, and 6. Conclusions and suggestions for future research are the subject of the final chapter.

Chapter 2 examines the demand for auditing as a monitoring technology in response to the existence of costly contracting among individuals. Specifically, we assert that the demand for audit services is derived from two general sources:

(1) the demand for the least-cost monitoring arrangement to facilitate owner-management contracts and thus enable current owners to capture the benefits of specialization, and

(2) the demand for the least-cost monitoring arrangement to facilitate intra-owner (e.g., shareholder-bondholder and current-potential shareholder) contracts and thus enable current owners to capture the benefits from issuing debt and additional equity securities.

Thus, a major role of auditors is to facilitate owner-management and intra-owner contracts by providing independent verification of the financial variables upon which these contracts are conditioned.

In Chapter 3, we analyze the nature of audit services. Prior auditing research has asserted that there are market failures associated with the provision of audited financial statements to the public.[8] Specifically, this literature has argued that auditing possesses the attributes of a public good, with an associated free rider-type externality. We argue that self-interested individuals have incentives to capture the benefits from auditing by devising arrangements which internalize any externalities. To the extent that the costs and benefits of audited financial statements are internalized by current owners, the decision to purchase audit services is conceptually identical to any other firm investment decision. In other words, audit services are likely to possess significant private good aspects. To the extent that audit services possess significant private good aspects, we can legitimately model the benefits from contracting for audit services as accruing to the client's shareholders.

Another common assertion about auditing which is explored in Chapter 3 is that the output of the audit process is infinitely costly to observe.[9] We argue that, if this were so, firms would not contract for audit services because they would be unable (at any cost) to determine whether or not they had, in fact, been audited. If the exchange of a good or service is sufficiently important to consumers, and some attribute of that good or service is very costly to measure, then self-interested, maximizing individuals will devise arrangements whereby other (less costly to observe) attributes serve as a surrogate for the attribute of interest. This will occur because of the existence of unexploited gains to such a strategy. One possible surrogate for audit output is auditor brand name. In

Chapter 3, we discuss the market forces which enable the brand name mechanism to signal audit quality, where direct observation of quality is costly.

An auditor's brand name, i.e., his professional reputation, is intimately linked to the extent to which he is perceived to be independent from his clients. In Chapter 4, we examine the potential benefits of auditor-client independence. The existence of potential benefits to auditor independence provides auditors and clients with the incentive to contract in a manner which enables both parties to capture these benefits. There are, however, certain exogenous factors in the exchange of audit services which inherently impair auditor independence by creating a material financial interest in clients. These factors are:

(1) The presence of significant learning-by-doing advantages (high start-up costs) in the provision of audit services, and

(2) The presence of positive transactions costs of changing auditors.

In Chapter 4, we present a model of the auditor's fee structure problem which predicts that, in the presence of (1) and (2) and of competition among auditors, auditors will "low-ball" on first time audits. We then analyze the implications of this theory for auditor independence and for extant regulation pertaining to audit fees and changes of auditor.

In Chapter 5, the model is extended to incorporate the auditor's choice of the number of audit clients and the client's choice of the length of the auditor-client relationship. This model highlights the importance of an auditor's other clients in the maintenance of audit quality. Intuitively, while the existence of future economic interest in a given client impairs auditor independence with respect to that client, the existence of future economic interest in other clients serves as a "collateral bond" to guarantee audit quality. Testable implications about changes in auditor concentration over time are developed. In addition, testable implications for the rate at which client firms change auditors are formulated and we also review extant evidence bearing on these predictions.

In Chapter 6, we introduce potential learning-by-doing advantages at the industry level. This extended model generates additional predictions about auditor specialization by client industry. Specifically, the Chapter 6 model predicts that, subsequent to an increase in industry level learning-by-doing advantages, auditors will have the incentive to increase (decrease) the number of industry clients if their relative cost advantages increase (decrease). Extant empirical evidence on auditor specialization by client industry is reviewed. Finally, conclusions and recommendations for future research are presented in Chapter 7.

2

Corporate Contracting Relationships and the Demand for Audit Services as a Monitoring Device

In this chapter, we examine two general sources of the derived demand for audit services. We assert that audit services are demanded because:

(1) They facilitate owner-management contractual arrangements by which original firm owners may capture potential benefits[1] from specialization, i.e., from the separation of ownership and control, and

(2) They facilitate intra-owner (implicit and explicit) contracts by which original owners may capture potential benefits[2] from issuing debt and equity securities.[3]

In this framework, audit services are demanded because they economize on the transactions costs of contracting among the various groups of individuals known as the "firm." Jensen and Meckling [1976] characterize the firm as "simply one form of legal fiction which serves as a nexus for contracting relationships" (p. 311). Viewed in this broad context, firms may be partitioned into various sets of contracting parties including shareholders, bondholders and other creditors, customers, managers and financial auditors. The contracts which define the various relationships, for example managerial remuneration agreements and bond covenants, are based in part upon accounting numbers. A major role of auditors is to facilitate contracting by providing independent verification of the financial variables upon which the other contractual relationships are conditioned.

Jensen and Meckling, Watts [1977], Benston [1979], and Watts and Zimmerman [March 1979, July 1979] argue that audited financial statements are demanded because they reduce agency costs. According to Jensen and Meckling, agency costs may arise when "one or more persons (the principal(s)) engage another person (the agent) to perform some service on their behalf which involves delegating some decision making authority to the agent" (p. 308). Agency costs are defined by Jensen and Meckling to be the sum of

(1) the monitoring expenditures by the principal,
(2) the bonding expenditures by the agent, and
(3) the residual loss.

The principal will wish to design an incentive structure for the agent which will, insofar as is cost-effective, reward those actions by the agent which are in the principal's own self interest. In addition, the principal may incur positive monitoring costs to assure himself of the agent's actions. Bonding expenditures are the costs to the agent of those actions which he takes to convince the principal that he will perform (or has performed) as promised. For example, an agent may put up a collateral bond which is forfeitable if the agent is discovered to have "cheated" the principal. The residual loss engendered by the agency relationship is defined by Jensen and Meckling as follows:

> In most agency relationships the principal and the agent will incur positive monitoring and bonding costs (non-pecuniary as well as pecuniary), and in addition there will be some divergence between the agent's decisions and those decisions which would maximize the welfare of the principal. The dollar equivalent of the reduction in welfare experienced by the principal due to this divergence is also a cost of the agency relationship, and we refer to this latter cost as the "residual loss." (p. 308)[4]

In this chapter, we wish to briefly examine two decisions by the owners of a firm:

(1) the decision to hire a professional manager, i.e., an individual who possesses a comparative advantage in managing firms, and
(2) the decision to raise additional capital (either debt or equity securities).

The first decision is the subject of Section 2.1.; the second is discussed in Section 2.2. In order to characterize these decisions, assume that a group of original owners (shareholders of the firm) is endowed with the property rights to a particular investment project. This productive opportunity may be a unique one, in the sense that it may represent a positive net present value investment, i.e., be specialized to the original owners. Both capital and labor markets are assumed to be ex ante competitive, i.e., initially, perfect substitutes exist for managers and for any security which the firm issues. Agency costs, as outlined earlier, are assumed to be present in owner-management and intra-owner contractual relationships. Specifically, conflicts of interest are likely to arise in the contractual relationship between owners (as principals) and managers (as agents) and between current and potential owners. Owner-manager conflicts of interest are the subject of the following section.

2.1 Owner-Management Contracting

In an agency cost framework, monitoring is demanded because it facilitates owner-manager contracts and thus enables the original owners to capture the benefits of specialization, i.e., the separation of ownership and control.[5] Firm owners (shareholders, bondholders, etc.) delegate the day-to-day operation of business activity to professional managers, individuals who possess a comparative advantage in overseeing firms' productive and distributive activities. These individuals, because of their daily involvement in firm operations, acquire another type of comparative advantage, specific knowledge of the financial details of the firm's transactions with outsiders and within its own organizational structure. Since the firm's owners are isolated from these events (and usually own a relatively small share of the firm and do not possess a comparative advantage in monitoring), they find it prohibitively costly to observe them directly. Therefore, they generally rely upon management to summarize and report the occurrence of transactions. The information asymmetry between owners and managers, however, provides managers with both the incentive and the opportunity to bias reports on its own performance in its favor. This problem is exacerbated when management's compensation is explicitly contingent upon the results of its operation of the firm.

Because of the potential for biased reporting by management, some (costly) monitoring arrangement will generally be optimal. The monitoring arrangement selected will be the one which minimizes the total costs of owner-management contracting. Since monitoring is itself costly, it will minimze, not remove these agency costs. Competition among managers will assure that the minimum cost monitoring technology is chosen because it is the one which will enable them to earn zero economic profits at equilibrium; any other monitoring arrangement will imply that unexploited gains from contracting are available to owners and managers. Competition in the labor market will force managers to exploit these gains. Competition among managers will also ensure that the benefits from monitoring will accrue entirely to current owners, because the benefits (above cost) to managers will be competed away. Fama [1980] argues that competition in the market for managerial services will eliminate (not simply minimize) agency costs. For Fama's argument to hold, the managerial market must be sufficiently perfect such that it essentially supplies costless monitoring of management. As long as monitoring is a costly activity, rational agents will employ the chosen monitoring alternative(s) until agency costs are minimized, not removed.

The monitoring arrangement which we generally observe for owner-manager contracts is that firm managers prepare financial statements to which independent auditors attest.[6] According to Jensen and Meckling, the manager's comparative cost advantage in supplying information about the firm underlies this arrangement:

> Suppose, for example, that the bondholders (or outside equity holders) would find it worthwhile to produce detailed financial statements such as those contained in the usual published accounting reports as a means of monitoring the manager. If the manager himself can produce such information at lower costs than they (perhaps because he is already collecting much of the data they desire for his own internal decision making purposes), it would pay him to agree in advance to incur the cost of providing such reports and to have their accuracy testified to by an independent outside auditor. (pp. 338-39)

The persistence of this arrangement, both with and without the presence of government regulation, suggests that it is an important monitoring arrangement.

It would be erroneous, however, to conclude that the provision of audited financial statements was the universal least-cost monitoring technology, prior to disclosure regulation. Benston [1975], for example, finds that "In 1926, all of the New York Stock Exchange listed corporations published balance sheets and net income, fifty-five percent disclosed sales, forty-five percent disclosed cost of goods sold, seventy-one percent disclosed depreciation and eighty-two percent were audited by CPAs" (p. 254). Since audited financial statements were not universally supplied, even by the largest listed firms, we can conclude that this monitoring technology was not the least-cost arrangement in all cases. It may be that regulation requires more monitoring (and/or monitoring of a different sort) than would be demanded otherwise. In the presence of disclosure regulation, the demand for audit services as a response to agency costs becomes more complex, because the observed phenomenon may not be the minimum cost alternative, absent the regulation. A complete positive theory of auditing which explains the existence and form of disclosure regulation is beyond the scope of this study.

2.2 Intra-Owner Contracting

Abstracting from the decision to hire a professional manager, we now examine the decision to raise additional capital in order to finance the investment project. The original owners of the property rights to the productive opportunity may decide to raise additional capital by selling either equity or debt securities. Presumably, if original owners decide to issue additional securities of either type, there are potential benefits to be gained from raising capital. However, potential problems may arise if the current owners possess more information about the project that potential suppliers of capital, and it is costly to reveal and authenticate this information. For example, the original owners may have a comparative advantage in assessing the "uniqueness" of the project. The information asymmetry between current and potential owners (either shareholders or bondholders) provides current shareholders with the incentive to disclose their information in order to raise new capital at the most advantageous rate. But the potential for false disclosure by the current owners implies that certification by an independent party may have value. Auditing is part of the certification process which we generally observe in the issuance of new securities.[7]

Absent independent verification, the discount rate at which the owners can raise additional capital will reflect the expectations of the outsiders. With independent verification of the current owners' claims, this rate will be lower to reflect the additional information. Thus, the presence of monitoring may enable current shareholders to undertake investment opportunities which otherwise would not be profitable (at higher discount rates). Auditing may enable current shareholders to capture these benefits by facilitating intra-owner contracting. The issuance of new equity is identical to the issuance of bonds; in both cases, the information disclosed by current shareholders and managers can affect the valuation of the firm's securities. Therefore, potential owners compensate current owners for information disclosure and authentication. For example, potential owners may compensate current owners for promising to disclose audited financial information about the firm by increased valuation of the firm's securities.

There is one important distinction between the issuance of debt and of additional equity securities. Bondholders are claimants to fixed amounts of the firm's earnings stream. Shareholders are residual claimants who retain the property rights to the decision making function. Since bondholders do not purchase the right to make firm decisions, they may be willing to compensate current owners for additional assurance about the decisions which shareholders and managers will make in future periods.[8] The potential opportunities for shareholders and managers to expropriate bondholder wealth are well known. For example, in the extreme, the shareholders could pay themselves a liquidating dividend and leave the bondholders with only an "empty shell." Or the shareholders could promise the bondholders that they would invest in low risk projects, and subsequently invest in high risk ones. Or the shareholders could issue unsubordinated debt that dilutes the claims of the earlier bondholders.[9] To the extent that bondholders foresee these strategies, they will lower the price of the bonds, and thus the bondholders will be "price-protected."

In addition to price adjustments, other alternatives are available to bondholders to protect themselves from expropriation attempts by shareholders. Bondholders can explicitly contract with shareholders to curtail shareholder strategies. The bond covenants we observe are complex documents which limit expropriation possibilities associated with real decisions by constraining accounting numbers. For example, dividends are usually limited to a specified percentage of net income, future debt issues may be required to be subordinated, certain financial ratios may be required to be maintained, etc.[10] The existence of bondholders may make some monitoring arrangement advantageous to shareholders. Audited financial statements are one possible monitoring technology. Current shareholders may benefit from auditing services because independent verification of the accounting numbers employed in bond covenants lowers monitoring costs. As Smith and Warner [1979] state:

> Potential bondholders estimate the costs associated with monitoring the firm to assure that the bond covenants have not been violated, and the estimate is reflected in the price when the bonds are sold. Since the value of the firm at the time the bonds are issued is influenced by anticipated monitoring costs, it is in the interests of the firm's owners to include contractual provisions which lower the costs of monitoring. For example, observed provisions often include the requirement that the firm supply audited annual financial statements to the bondholders. (p. 43)

Thus, the provision of audited financial statements may enable current shareholders to capture the benefits from the issuance of debt securities.

There is another source of potential benefits from auditing which accrue to the current shareholders. If it is costly for individuals to sort securities, i.e., to determine the "quality" of firm securities, then audited financial statements may have value to them as a sorting mechanism.[11] For simplicity, assume that there exist only two types of firms: those which have access to superior productive opportunities and those which do not. We label the first firms high quality firms and the others low quality firms. In addition, it is costly for individuals other than firm managers (who are assumed to own no securities of any firm) to determine the quality of firms. In the absence of any information, all firms would have the same market value. Therefore, unexploited gains exist to differentiation of high from low quality firms. The existence of potential gains provides individuals with the incentive to incur positive search costs by gathering information on all potential candidates for purchase. In addition, each potential owner of the firm's securities would have the incentive to incur search costs, and investor "oversearching," i.e., a duplication of effort, could result.

If the high quality firms could provide information about themselves at lower cost than potential investors, then investors would be willing to compensate these firms by paying a higher price for their securities. Thus, managers of high quality firms have incentives to disclose information about the firm. However, because of the information asymmetry between managers and current and potential owners, managers of low quality firms also have the incentive to misrepresent firm quality in order to capture the valuation impact. Because of this potential for misrepresentation by management, some type of authentication, such as auditing, may be demanded by potential investors. If an independent third party, upon whom investors could rely, were to certify management's representations, then sorting by firm quality would be facilitated. Sorting is valuable to investors because it better enables them to forecast and arrange the timing and amount of future cash flows. Thus, for example, when firms supply audited financial statements, individual investors may be made better off because

(1) Their earnings realizations are drawings from a high or a low quality group, rather than from a pooled group of securities, and

(2) They avoid the search costs associated with differentiating the firms themselves.

Individuals will compensate high quality firms who supply these benefits by paying a higher price for the firm's securities.

In the absence of information provision by firms, individuals may incur positive search costs because they are presumed to be aware that all firms sell for the same price, but there are quality differences among firms. An example of a similar case is milk cartons in supermarkets. Since all milk cartons sell for the same price, but are heterogeneous in quality, consumers may expend resources in attempts to determine which milk is the freshest. If, in addition to undated cartons of milk, manufacturers also supplied dated cartons, then consumers would be willing to compensate them for differentiation. In other words, with positive search costs, consumers would be willing to pay a higher price for the joint product, milk and information that the milk is fresh. At the same time, they would now be unwilling to pay the same price for fresh and non-fresh milk.[12] Or if, for another example, all theatre tickets sell for the same price, consumers will queue up to get the best seats. Waiting in line has a time cost to customers which the theatre owner is not capturing. Some of those customers would likely prefer to pay a higher price for reserved seats. As Barzel [1979] notes, in these situations

> Consumers will shop earlier to gain the best selection among heterogeneous units. Yet, as already noted, the inspection of items not subsequently purchased is a duplication of effort. This is a costly activity; therefore a consumer will not willingly offer as much for the item as he would have done, had he been spared the added cost. (p. 18)

By similar reasoning, we can infer that the provision of audited financial statements has value to investors, for which they will compensate high quality firms by paying a higher price for firm securities.

In the absence of disclosure regulation, firms supply information voluntarily if firm owners and managers believe that information provision will result in higher firm valuation. Firms which supply authenticated information voluntarily would most likely be high quality firms.[13] Absent mandated disclosure, non-disclosing firms will be "priced out" in the capital market to reflect investors' joint probability assessments that the firm is both high quality and a non-discloser. With mandated disclosure, low quality firms must incur the costs of identifying themselves as such. The issues of who gains and who loses from mandated information disclosure are beyond the scope of this study.

We can briefly summarize the discussion thus far: audit services are valuable to the extent that they reduce the costs of monitoring and therefore facilitate owner-manager and intra-owner contractual arrangements. Firm owners contract with management to operate the firm. Management formally reports the results of operations to shareholders via the firm's annual report (as well as informally through news releases, forecasts, etc.). In addition to equity securities, firms typically also issue debt securities; the associated bond covenants constrain accounting numbers to limit potential expropriation of bondholder wealth. Auditors supply current owners with independent verification of management-prepared financial statements, which are then generally made available to the public. By facilitating owner-management and intra-owner contracts, this arrangement may enable current owners to capture the benefits of cooperation. These potential benefits include increased firm efficiencies due to specialization and the ability to undertake investment opportunities which may not be profitable absent the provision of verified financial information by the current owners.

2.3 Who Bears the Cost of Audit Services?

In Sections 2.1 and 2.2, we argued that the benefits from optimal contracting accrue to the current owners of the property rights to firm productive opportunities. In this section, we examine the question: who bears the costs of contracting? As in earlier sections of the chapter, we continue to assume that a group of original owners (shareholders) has access to a positive net present value project (at a discount rate which fully reflects the owners' information set).[14] The owners are assumed to be faced with two decisions: the decision to hire a professional manager for the project, and the decision to raise additional capital by issuing debt or equity securities. At the same time these two decisions are made, the owners can also contract for audit services.

To the extent that auditing has value to the professional manager, he will compensate current owners by adjusting his wage. Assume that auditing is the minimum cost monitoring technology. If any other (less effective) monitoring technology is chosen, the manager's wage will be lowered to reflect his increased ability to consume perquisites, overstate net income, etc. Auditing will enable his negotiated wage to rise, relative to his wage under the next-best monitoring technology. That is, wages adjust so that it is to the manager's advantage to hire monitors of his own actions. Competition in the market for managerial services will limit the amount by which the manager's wage rises to that monetary amount which makes him just indifferent between

(1) His wage under the next-best monitoring technology combined with the perquisites he could consume under this arrangement, and

(2) The "with auditing" wage which enables a minimal amount of perquisites (since it is not, in general, cost-effective to remove all perquisite consumption).

The manager, however, will not be indifferent between the two strategies. Firm owners will strictly prefer the latter alternative because firm value will increase by the capital market's valuation of increased firm efficiency from employing the least-cost monitoring technology. Because of the owner's preferences for (2), competition among managers will ensure that (2) earns zero profits at equilibrium, while (1) represents unexploited gains to both owners and managers (as well as negative profits to managers at equilibrium). Therefore, both parties have incentives to contract until no unexploited gains (net of contracting costs) remain.

We turn now to the decision to issue additional securities to raise capital. Suppose that there are potential benefits to be gained from issuing debt. These benefits may be due to incentive effects, or to the differential tax treatment of debt and equity at the corporate level. These potential benefits give current owners the incentive to contract with potential bondholders in such a way as to capture the benefits. Potential bondholders will recognize shareholder strategies which serve to expropriate bondholders, and will discount the price of the bonds accordingly. As long as perfect substitutes exist for firm securities, the original owners will be forced to either voluntarily constrain their behavior or accept a lower price for the firm's bonds. Monitoring arrangements will lessen expected bondholder expropriations and thereby lower the interest rate which bondholders will demand. Suppose that auditing is the monitoring arrangement which minimizes the agency costs of shareholder-bondholder contracting. Efficient capital markets will ensure that the price the bondholders are willing to pay for the bonds will fully reflect the expected benefit of the audit to the bondholders. The interest rate on the firm's bonds will adjust until the bondholders are just indifferent between

(1) The lower interest rate combined with the presence of auditing, and

(2) A higher interest rate combined with the next-best monitoring technology.

Current shareholders will strictly prefer the former alternative because auditing is assumed to be the least-cost monitoring technology. In an efficient capital market, the firm's share price will fully reflect the net benefits of issuing bonds in the most efficient (least cost) manner. As for the bondholders, as long as the capital market is efficient and incorporates rational expectations, the bondholders are "price-protected." The price the bondholders are willing to pay for firm securities will fully reflect their expectations about potential shareholder expropriation strategies. On average, their ex post realizations will confirm their ex ante expectations, and bondholders will neither benefit nor suffer ex post.

The argument is symmetric for the issuance of new equity shares. To the extent that potential shareholders benefit from the firm's provision of audited financial statements, competition will force them to compensate current owners by adjusting the price they are willing to pay for the firm's securities. On the other hand, the existence of perfect substitutes for the firm's securities in the capital market will make new shareholders unwilling to pay an "abnormally" high price for equity shares. In other words, efficient capital markets will ensure that new shareholders earn no more than a normal (risk-adjusted) rate of return on their investment in the firm. Any abnormal gains from optimal contracting will accrue to the original owners of the property rights to firm productive opportunities.[16]

To summarize this section: we have argued that competition among managers, among bondholders, and among potential shareholders will ensure that these individuals will fully compensate current owners for the benefits conferred on them by the presence of auditing.[17] The remainder of the audit costs, as well as the benefits, accrue entirely to current shareholders. In the following chapter, we analyze some assertions about the nature of audit services which are commonly made in extant audit research.

3

On the Nature of Audit Services

Before modeling the equilibrium pricing of audit services, we should define precisely what is meant by the term, "audit services." The output of the audit process is an auditor's opinion on the "fairness" of management-prepared financial statements. The process by which the final product, audited financial statements, is produced is a joint process with inputs supplied by both auditor and client. For example, the client supplies the data input, management-prepared financial statements. The auditor then gathers additional evidence which either substantiates or refutes management's representations and which allows him to express an opinion as to the "fairness" of management's claims. The actual procedures employed in the audit process may vary across auditors and between engagements. According to Willingham and Carmichael [1975], "the nature of the audit procedures used may be varied. The audit procedures may be performed at different times during the year and the extent of the selected audit procedures may be increased or decreased" (p. 147). Thus the auditor can vary (1) the type of audit procedures, (2) the timing, and (3) the extent to which the procedure is employed. The actual audit procedures employed are recorded in the working papers, which are retained by the auditor and which serve as documentation of the nature, timing, and extent of audit procedures carried out on a given audit engagement.

The commodity which the auditor alone supplies is independent verification of management-prepared financial data. Associated with a given auditor's opinion is the confidence which consumers of audit services place in that opinion, i.e., an assessed probability that the financial statements do "fairly present" the client's financial condition.[1] This quality dimension is the user confidence associated with a given auditor's opinion. The quality dimension of a given level of audit services may be costly for consumers to evaluate. Prior auditing literature has asserted that audit quality is unobservable; prior auditing literature has also asserted that audit services are a public good with an associated free rider externality. These assertions, if true, pose serious questions about the validity of modeling audit services as (1) a private good, and (2) as a commodity which can serve as a basis for contracts between individuals.

18 The Nature of Audit Services

Because the formal models in Chapters 4, 5, and 6 characterize audit services as though (1) and (2) are appropriate, we examine these allegations in some detail in the present chapter before proceeding to the formal models.

In Section 3.1, we discuss the common assertion that audit services are a public good. We argue that, to the extent that auditing is demanded as a monitoring technology, the firm's investment in audit services results in increased firm efficiency. Efficient capital markets will ensure that current owners of the firm are compensated for this increased efficiency by increased valuation of the firm. Furthermore, we argue that intra-shareholder free riders are effectively prevented because joint ownership combined with proportional sharing effectively removes externalities. We conclude that auditing possesses significant private good aspects, and that, in the formal models of later chapters, it is appropriate to model these aspects of audit services as a private good.

In Section 3.2, we examine another common assertion in the auditing literature: that the output of the audit process is unobservable. We argue that, were this the case, firms would not contract for audit services. Therefore, while the quality of an audit may be costly to observe, it cannot be infinitely costly or audits would not be supplied. We argue that one mechanism which serves to signal audit quality when direct observation is costly is the brand name of the auditor. We discuss extant institutional arrangements in the market for audit services which impose a minimum level of audit quality. We conclude the section by discussing how auditor brand name may serve to signal quality above the minimum standard where demand for audit services is heterogeneous. Finally, in Section 3.3., we review extant auditing literature which discusses auditor brand name. In addition, we describe two models of costly quality determination from the economics literature which serve to illustrate how the brand name mechanism operates.

3.1 Audit Services and Free Rider Problems

Several auditing researchers (see, for example, Ng [1978], Magee [1979], Barefield and Beck [1979], and Dopuch and Simunic [1979]) have asserted that audit services possess a public good aspect with an associated free rider externality.[2] Ng, for instance, characterizes the output of the audit process as the probability of detection of a material error and of non-compliance with generally accepted accounting principles (GAAP). Ng asserts that

> ... the fact that one stockholder enjoys a particular level of the probability of detection does not preclude the enjoyment of the same level of the probability of detection by other stockholders or potential stockholders of the same firm. This is why apples are considered a private commodity while audit services are considered a public good. (p. 109)

The Nature of Audit Services 19

This analysis implies that both current and potential shareholders (i.e., in the limit, any individual) can "consume" the benefits of an audit without decreasing the benefits available to all other individuals. Ng further asserts that, for each current and potential owner, there is a free rider problem insofar as

> Everyone wants the others to pay for the cost of the audit, because once the financial statements are audited, those who have paid cannot bar those who have not paid from enjoying the benefits. (p. 110)

Before proceeding further, we should distinguish between a public good and a public good problem. All economic goods are likely to exhibit some public good and some private good aspects. For example, physically attractive houses can be simultaneously "enjoyed" by many individuals; however, theorists generally ignore the public good aspect by modeling housing services as a private good. The question of whether a good is more appropriately modeled as public or private ultimately rests on the empirical validity of each model's predictions. As argued by Watts and Milne [1977]:

> The assumptions of all theoretical models are necessarily caricatures of reality—they are not universally correct. The ultimate test of alternative assumptions, of alternative models, is empirical. We choose between alternative assumptions (models) on the basis of which one provides the best predictions. (p. 1)

While the ultimate test of a model is empirical, several theoretical arguments support the conclusion that auditing possesses significant private good aspects.

In Chapter 2, it was argued that, if auditing is the least-cost monitoring technology, the capital market rationally expects a firm which engages an auditor to choose a more efficient set of production/investment decisions.[3] In other words, the value of the firm will reflect the decision to employ that monitoring arrangement which minimizes the total costs of contracting. The "benefit" due to auditing is this value increment which, in the presence of competitive capital and labor markets, accrues entirely to the current owners of the "firm."[4] To the extent that the presence of an audit benefits managers competition in the market for professional managers will assure that managers fully compensate current owners by adjusting their wage. To the extent that auditing confers benefits on potential shareholders (bondholders), efficient capital markets will ensure that potential owners compensate current owners by adjusting the price of the firm's shares (bonds). In short, competition among managers, among bondholders, and among potential shareholders will ensure that these individuals will fully compensate current owners for the benefits conferred on them by the presence of auditing.

To the extent that the "benefits" of an audit are increased firm efficiencies which are correctly anticipated by the capital market, then non-purchasing outsiders (anyone other than current shareholders) are effectively excluded from sharing these benefits. In other words, the benefits of the audit are effectively tied in to ownership of the firm's shares.[5] Any remaining "benefits" from an audit, if not captured by the firm, must entail transactions costs of capture which exceed potential gains from capture. An interesting analogy is provided by parking lots in shopping centers. Generally stores do not charge directly for parking services. However, economic analysis would suggest that the price of parking services is tied in to the products which the store sells to consumers. What then of the shopper who merely window-shops, but does not buy? If many such free-riders exist, the store loses significant revenues from parking services. On the other hand, installing fences and turnstiles, hiring parking attendants, etc., is costly. If we observe free parking, we can conclude that the costs of charging a separate fee exceed the expected capturable benefits. Similarly, if absent disclosure regulation, we observe "free" financial statements, we can conclude that the costs of charging a fee exceed the capturable benefits.

We have argued that, under certain assumptions, the benefits from contracting for audit services are effectively tied in to share ownership. It remains to be demonstrated that within the current shareholder group there is no free rider problem. All current shareholders may wish to enjoy the benefits of audit services without paying for them. In fact, Ng [1978] asserts that the alleged public good aspect of audit services is likely to cause disagreement within the current shareholder group about the sharing arrangement for audit fees. He claims that shareholder disagreement over audit fees may result in a "market failure" with an attendant nonoptimal resource allocation:

> If investors are left to themselves, they may be unable to agree on how to share the cost of an audit. As a result, it is possible that little, if any, of auditing services will be acquired, although it may be to each stockholder's benefit to have an audit. This is an instance in which the market mechanism, if left to itself, may result in a less than optimal allocation of resources. (p. 110)

This argument has virtually nothing to do with the asserted public good aspect of audit services; it would apply equally well to any other investment decision. To see this, substitute the word "machine" for "audit" and "audit services" in the above quotation. Investors, i.e., current shareholders, however, are not "left to themselves" because a proportional sharing rule is in effect for all decisions.[6] The group as a whole (the "firm") contracts for audit services and no "holdouts" are possible. It is well known in economics that joint ownership with proportional sharing is sufficient (but not necessary) to remove externalities which prevent the efficient utilization of resources.

To see how joint ownership by one individual removes externalities, suppose that there are many individual owners of small (equal-sized) plots of farm land, each of equal productivity. Let us also assume that the total productivity of the n plots is unknown, but can be verified by an independent expert at some cost. In a world of costly information, the expert's opinion has value to the landowners because it enables the land value to reflect its certified productivity. Now, by contracting with the expert to certify the total productivity of the n plots, each owner also certifies the productivity of his own plot (assumed to be equal to $1/n$). If, by contracting for verification of the total productivity, an owner reveals this datum to all other owners, individual owners will have reduced incentives to contract for certification. Yet verification has value to these individuals. Therefore, we can infer that arrangements will be sought by these individuals which will enable them to capture that value. One possible arrangement is joint ownership by one individual.

If one individual owned the n plots of farm land, he would fully internalize the costs and benefits of verification. This is true because this one individual would bear all the costs of verification and, similarly, he would reap all the benefits. No free rider problem would remain, because the property rights to all benefits have been fully assigned to the one owner.

Similarly, the cost and benefits could be fully internalized if the group adopted an ex ante sharing rule which prevented distribution problems among many owners. In other words, when one owner can steal from another, the "jointness," by itself, will not solve the problem. Note that the purpose of a well-specified sharing rule is precisely to remove this dissipation. A proportional sharing rule which is specified ex ante is just such a rule. In other words, if the group as a whole contracts for verification and "holdouts" are effectively prevented because proportional sharing is in effect, then no free rider-type externality exists among current owners. A similar arrangement is characteristic of the modern "firm," i.e., the firm which contracts for audit services already exists in a form which is sufficient to fully internalize material free rider externalities. Thus our simple example is similar to the phenomenon of interest. We conclude that no significant free rider problems can be present within the current shareholder group.

One important distinction exists between the firm's decision to purchase audit services and the land example above. In the land example, the total productivity of the land is fixed, i.e., is not affected by verification. Auditing, however, may increase total firm productivity by providing current owners with the incentive to make "better" production/investment decisions. To see this distinction, assume that firm owners know more about their production/investment decisions than do outsiders. In order for the capital market to reward owners for "better" decisions, it must be aware of these decisions. Current owners have the incentive to disclose their decisions in order to capture the valuation benefits. But the information asymmetry between current and potential owners provides current owners with the incentives for false disclosure. Verificiation by an independent party may help to assure potential owners that current owners will disclose the "truth," even if it is "bad news," i.e., even if it has a negative impact on current shareholder wealth. Thus, audited financial statements provide verification of the firm's decisions and, therefore, increased incentives for firm's owners to make "better" decisions. This "productive" impact of auditing is identical to the productive impact of signalling noted by Barzel [1977].

To summarize this section: we argued that the costs and benefits of contracting for audit services are internalized to the extent that

(1) efficient capital and labor markets assure that the benefits of contracting for audit services accrue entirely to the current shareholders, and because

(2) joint ownership combined with ex ante proportional sharing is a sufficient condition to fully internalize material free rider-type externalities.

Audit services, therefore, are likely to possess significant private good aspects. We conclude that standard economic analysis for private goods is applicable to audit services demanded as a monitoring device; the firm's decision with respect to investment in such audit services is conceptually identical to any other investment decision and is therefore subject to the same cost-benefit calculus.[7] In the following section, we analyze another common assertion in the auditing literature: that the output of the audit process is unobservable.

3.2 The Observability of Audit Ouptut and the Brand Name Mechanism

Prior auditing research (see, for example, Ng [1978], Kaplan [1978], Magee [1979], Barefield and Beck [1979], and Dopuch and Simunic [1979]) has also asserted that audit output is not observable (at any finite cost). Ng [1978], for example, argues that

> ... unobservability refers to the fact that the output of the audit production function, the probability of detection, is not observable to current and potential shareholders ... Unobservability of the probability of detection suggests that no market price for this would exist. . . (p. 108)

The alleged unobservability of audit output leads Ng to conclude that audit fees will be based on auditor inputs rather than on audit output ("no market price for this would exist"). And yet we observe fixed fee structures for the exchange of audit services, i.e., a pre-arranged flat fee paid for an audit, not for x hours of auditor time inputs. More importantly, owner-management and intra-owner contracts are often conditioned on the presence of an audit.

In this section, we argue that the notion of unobservability which persists in current economic characterizations of the market for audit services is both

(1) incomplete, and
(2) inconsistent with the observation that the presence of an audit serves as a basis for intra-owner, owner-management, and owner-auditor contractual agreements.

We reconcile this inconsistency by arguing that, while audit quality may be costly to observe, it cannot be the case that it is unobservable, or firms would not contract for audits. We characterize audit output as independent verification with an associated quality dimension, i.e., the confidence level which consumers of audit services place in the auditor's opinion.[8] This quality dimension may be costly to observe, but it cannot be infinitely costly to do so.[9]

When observation of audit quality is costly, innovative individuals will have the incentive to devise market arrangements which enable quality to be evaluated by consumers. It is in the self-interest of such individuals to devise these arrangements, because otherwise potential gains from exchange would go unexploited. For example, if some mechanism were not available to provide clients with assurance that auditors will perform the services for which they contract, then clients would not contract with auditors. No audits would be demanded if audit output were unobservable, or as Ng [1978] correctly points out, "a basic observation in economics is that no contracts contingent on an event can be made if at the time of execution either of the contracting parties does not know whether the specified contingency has occurred or not" (p. 101).

If audit output were unobservable, i.e., infinitely costly to observe, then clients would not contract with auditors because it would not be possible at any finite cost for clients to know whether they were receiving the audit services for which they contracted. If audit output were unobservable, how would clients know whether they were receiving any audit services at all? We observe clients contracting with auditors to supply independent verification of management-prepared financial statements. We also observe owner-manager and intra-owner contracts conditioned on the audited statements. Therefore, we can infer that audit output (or a surrogate) must be observable or contracts contingent upon independent verification would not be feasible. If none is observable, there will be no audit.

When observation of product quality is costly, we have argued that self-interested, maximizing individuals have incentives to devise contractual arrangements which enable quality to be evaluated. One such arrangement is for producer brand name to signal the quality of a product to consumers. Specifically, auditor brand name may serve as a signal of the quality of audit services. If this is the case, then auditors will expend real resources to establish "brand names" in order to economize on costly search by the consumers of audit services.[10,11] In this section, we discuss extant institutional arrangements which (exogenously) guarantee a minimum standard of audit quality. We then discuss the use of the brand name mechanism to signal quality which exceeds the minimum standard, where explicit contractual provisions may be relatively more costly to enforce.

Audit quality, i.e., the user confidence attached to a given type of opinion from a given auditor, may be very costly for consumers to evaluate, not only ex ante, but ex post as well. In other words, even "consumption" of an audit may not reveal its quality.[12] It may be difficult to evaluate audit quality over time for any given auditor, not to mention cross-sectionally across all potential auditors in the market. A duplication of effort is likely to occur, since every consumer would have to engage in a costly search process. Furthermore, auditors have more information about the actual procedures employed on a given audit than outsiders are likely to gather by observation, i.e., an information asymmetry exists between auditors and consumers of their services. Therefore, we would expect to observe auditors signalling their personal assessments of audit quality to consumers. One method of signalling audit quality is to expend resources on the establishment of a professional reputation, or brand name.[13] Of course, in order for signalling to occur, economic incentives to signal must exist. In other words, auditors who have established brand names can be expected to earn a return on their investment in reputation, i.e., to charge higher audit fees.

If the establishment of a brand name is a response to client search costs, we would expect auditors to specialize in a stable level of audit quality both across clients and over time. A stable quality level would economize on search costs which consumers would otherwise incur to evaluate audit quality. As a practical matter, we would expect the quality supplied by different auditors or classes of auditors to differ cross-sectionally. In general, clients with differential costs of contracting will demand differing levels of audit quality in which various auditors (or classes of auditors) will specialize. This effect may partially explain the repeated observation that firms going public for the first time often switch to "Big Eight" accounting firms.[14] In any case, if auditors do specialize in a stable level of quality across clients and through time, then observation of the auditor brand name aids consumers to assess the quality of audit services supplied. Individuals have incentives to substitute a (less costly) surrogate for audit output so that contracts can be negotiated contingent upon a specified variable.[15]

The brand name mechanism is a costly form of implicit contract. If we observe this mechanism in the exchange of audit services, we can infer that it is the least-cost method of guaranteeing quality in at least some cases. It is still, however, a costly mechanism. Barzel [1979] isolates three types of costs associated with the brand name phenomenon: the establishment of a reputation; the cost of quality control to assure product uniformity; and the maintenance of uniformity when external pressures call for a change. The costs associated with the brand name mechanism of signalling quality are a component of the costs of providing audit services in a world where information is not costless. They are only "inefficient" in a Nirvana world where information is costless. As mentioned earlier, such a world would not only imply no brand-naming, but also a zero demand for (costly) auditing as well.

The function of the brand name mechanism is to signal audit quality, where quality is costly to observe. This function may also be accomplished through an institutional arrangement, such as a guarantee by the government (as with government-insured savings accounts) or licensing by a professional organization (such as the American Bar Association). The market for audit services is characterized by the existence of institutions which impose a minimum level of audit quality. First, generally accepted auditing standards (GAAS) mandate a minimum level of audit quality by constraining auditor inputs.[16] Second, at the individual auditor level, in order to qualify for the designation of certified public accountant, auditors must meet minimum certification standards: they must satisfy education and experience requirements (which vary by state) and, in addition, they must pass the Uniform CPA Exam. This examination is required by all 54 United States jurisdictions and is administered by the American Institute of Certified Public Accountants (AICPA).

Substandard performance at the individual level is subject to professional sanctions by the individual's state board of accountancy, the AICPA and potentially to discipline by the SEC and the courts. Professional sanctions principally consist of public chastisement of the individual. This mechanism is effective because, if an individual auditor is publicly discredited, the loss of human capital he sustains is likely to be large. Should an auditing firm be discovered to have "cheated" on audit quality, professional sanctions can be imposed at both the individual and the firm level. Auditing firms are generally organized as continuing professional partnerships. This form of organization serves to put the partners' personal wealth, as well as their human capital, at stake.[17]

Until recently, only individuals were members of the AICPA and thus subject to disciplinary action by the Institute. Discipline of auditing firms had been performed by the SEC and the courts. In September 1977, the AICPA Council made significant changes in the structure of the Institute. Firms are now eligible for membership in one or both of two sections: an SEC practice section and a private practice section. The primary differences between the two practice sections are the requirements for a Public Oversight Board, mandatory audit partner rotation, the filing of certain public information with respect to

SEC client composition, and certain restrictions on the provision of management advisory services. In addition, these two sections can impose certain sanctions on member firms, which were previously not available to the AICPA. For the detailed differences between the two sections, see Appendix A.

Prior to the restructuring of the AICPA, institutional arrangements within the auditing profession served to mandate one level of minimum quality auditing. Differentiation of quality above that minimum level was left to the individual audit firms. We now observe an institutional arrangement which differentiates between those audit firms which practice before the SEC and those firms which do not, i.e., two levels of institutionally-imposed minimum standards exist. Differentiation of audit quality above those levels is accomplished by the audit firms themselves.

We have seen that institutional arrangements serve to impose a minimum quality standard for audit services. The Cohen Report asserts that "honest" clients will demand only minimum quality audit services:

> To a fully competent and honest financial manager, the major result of the audit, a "clean opinion" on the company's financial statements, is of little direct value. It merely satisfies a requirement. If the financial manager has confidence in the quality of the financial statements he has prepared, he will appropriately attempt to purchase audit services at as low a price as is reasonably possible. (p. 107)

This assertion is clearly erroneous because it assumes that managers can costlessly reveal their actions to all.[18] If this were true, not only would firms purchase the minimum quality audit services but, with costly auditing, they would prefer to purchase none at all. As discussed in Chapter 2, audit services are demanded as monitoring devices because of the potential conflicts between owners and managers as well as those among different classes of security holders. If negotiating and enforcing contracts were costless (i.e., if managers could costlessly reveal their actions), no such derived demand would exist for audit services. In the absence of government regulation, no (costly) auditing would be demanded by firms. This is clearly not the case, as several authors, notably Benston [1969, July 1969] and Watts and Zimmerman [July 1979] have shown.

Differential costs of contracting (across clients or across time for a given client) imply a heterogeneous demand for audit services. For example, publicly held firms may demand a different level of audit services than do privately held firms. Clients who face differentially higher contracting costs may demand a level of audit quality which exceeds the minimum quality standard. Given a positive demand for audit services that exceed the institutionally-enforced minimum standards, how do auditors and clients contract for these services? One mechanism which enables clients and auditors to contract for higher-than-minimum quality audit services is the auditor brand name mechanism.[19]

The brand name mechanism is similar to an arrangement where the auditor puts up a collateral bond, which is forfeitable in full if the auditor supplies less "assurance" than he contracted for ex ante. We do not currently observe an explicit collateral bond arrangement for the exchange of audit services,[20] perhaps because of the "reverse cheating" problem. "Reverse cheating" refers to the client's incentive to (opportunistically) claim auditor cheating in order to expropriate the collateral bond, i.e., to effect a direct wealth transfer from auditors to clients. "Reverse cheating" occurs because clients can capture the proceeds from a collateral bond; it is not as severe a problem with the brand name mechanism because of the auditor-specific nature of the brand name. Clients have a lessened incentive to engage in "reverse cheating" because, while they may be able to impose a loss of brand name on auditors, clients cannot capture direct economic benefits from the loss.[21]

The mechanism which makes both the collateral bond arrangement and the brand name effective in signalling quality is the threat of capital loss if the auditor gets caught "cheating" on quality.[22] In the first case, the auditor stands to lose the collateral bond. In the second, he stands to lose the present value of the future audit fees he can charge due to his professional reputation as an auditor. He will lose this wealth equivalent because of clients' (and potential clients') ability to withdraw future business from the auditor if they determine that the auditor has supplied a lower-than-promised audit quality. The enforcement mechanism is effective because a capital loss can be imposed on the auditor if he loses his brand name. The repeat business mechanism is not a perfect one if it is difficult ex post to determine whether "cheating" has occurred. For example, audit failures may only become public information after a time lag. Since it is costly for clients to observe auditor opportunism, we would not expect the brand name mechanism to remove all quality depreciation by auditors.

Because of its reliance on repeat sales in the future as an enforcement arrangement, the brand name mechanism is subject to potential "last period" problems. If audit output is very costly to observe, auditors will depreciate quality in the last period because there are no future sales to lose. Higher than minimum quality audit services will not be supplied in the last period. But if only minimum quality is supplied in the last period, the repeat business mechanism will not be effective in the second-to-last period, and so on. Thus, in the absence of some settling-up mechanism, the solution will unravel and higher than minimum quality will not be supplied.[23]

However, if there are potential benefits to be gained from brand-naming in earlier periods, we would expect to observe individuals designing contracts which minimize the impact of last period problems (e.g., transferability of brand name, some form of ex post "settling up," etc.). The structuring of audit firms as continuing partnerships may be partially explained as an attempt to avoid last period problems. A partner's interest can be sold upon his retirement; thus he has the incentive to maintain the firm's brand name, since he can capture the benefits at the time of sale. Such is not the case with employees who own no stake in the firm; with these employees, some sort of ex post "settling up" mechanism can be expected to appear (see Fama [1980]).

In summary, in this section we have examined the question of whether audit output is infinitely costly to observe. We characterized audit output as independent verification of management-prepared financial statements, with an associated quality dimension. Audit quality cannot be infinitely costly to observe (because then no audits would be supplied), but it is likely to be very costly to observe. When the object of interest is very costly to observe, consumers will rely on less-costly surrogates. We argued that one potential surrogate for audit quality is the brand name of the auditor. We then briefly examined some economic forces which enable auditor brand name to signal audit quality in the exchange of audit services. In the following section, we review current auditing research which has discussed the importance of auditor brand name. We also describe two models of costly quality determination from the economics literature.

3.3 The Brand Name Phenomenon: Literature Review

Prior auditing research has argued that the brand name phenomenon may be an important factor in the exchange of audit services. Watts and Zimmerman [July 1979], for example, claim that the function of professional bodies such as the AICPA is to differentiate high quality auditors from those of lower quality. Watts and Zimmerman cite historical sources which claim that

> There is casual evidence that large audit firms have established brand names. Firms were jealous of their name in the nineteenth century. For example, at the end of the nineteenth century, Price, Waterhouse & Company was reluctant to allow their first representatives in the U.S. (Jones and Caesar) to use the firm name for fear of damage to their reputation [DeMond, 1951, p. 16]. (p. 42)

Dopuch and Simunic [1979] also mention the potential importance of brand name in those situations where quality determination is costly. They assert that "service industries in general rely upon reputation to obtain 'sales', perhaps because of the difficulty in assessing the quality of services" (p. 15). While Watts and Zimmerman and Dopuch and Simunic mention the potential importance of auditor brand name, neither paper provides a model of how the brand name mechanism might serve to guarantee audit quality.

Benston [1979] examines the brand name phenomenon in more detail than do the other two papers. Benston asserts that the joint product which auditors supply is their technical expertise and their professional reputation. Benston then argues that the auditor's self interest is sufficient to prevent him from depreciating the quality of his services:

> ... those who employ the public accountant can rely on the accountant's self interest in acquiring and maintaining a reputation for integrity and expertise. Should a public accountant be found to have been suborned (or to have been negligent or inexpert in conducting an audit, given the fees charged), other clients and users of the client's financial statements will have reason to doubt the accountant's integrity or his/her ability to perform an audit. Therefore, the monetary cost (ex ante) to public accountants who accept bribes or who conduct audits incompetently is the present value of the loss of profits from current and future clients, times the probability of discovery and exposure. (pp. 5-6)

Benston's analysis does not suffice to rule out quality depreciation by auditors: it only states that the expected marginal cost to the auditor of "cheating" is the present value of the loss of future fees due to "cheating" times the probability of being caught. A complete analysis would also specify the marginal benefits to the auditor from depreciating audit quality. Both the marginal costs and benefits of auditor opportunism must be specified before any conclusion can be drawn about the extent of such opportunism.

While the auditing literature has but few references to auditor brand name, there are several economics papers which deal with costly quality determination and brand naming in general. In what follows, we review two models from the economics literature which deal with costly quality determination. These two models serve to highlight market arrangements which enable quality to be supplied when observation of quality is costly to consumers.

In general, if quality depreciation is costly to observe, arrangements which minimize, not remove, quality depreciation will be sought by the parties which potentially benefit from the maintenance of audit quality. Darby and Karni [1973] provide an analysis of the optimal amount of fraud for credence goods (goods for which quality determination is costly, even post-purchase). In their model, a repair services firm faces stochastic demand for services under two scenarios. In the first scenario, the length of the queue is zero; in the second scenario, it is positive. In the Darby and Karni model, if quality information is infinitely costly, then the amount of fraud is limited by the difference between the price of a new unit and the salvage value of the old unit.

The type of fraud that occurs in the Darby and Karni model varies depending on the number of customers in the queue. If no customers are waiting, fraud takes the form of prescribing more repair services than are necessary and of prolonging the repair time on a given job. With customers waiting in the queue, fraud can be either (1) reporting but not providing repair services, or (2) reselling used parts as new. Darby and Karni's model implies that "the higher the anticipated value of future profits from a customer, the smaller the tendency to defraud him" (p. 74). In other words, the threat of withdrawal of future business is the mechanism which serves to deter fraud. And the greater the value of that future business, the more it serves to curtail fraudulent practices. Therefore, one prediction of the Darby and Karni model is that regular customers will be defrauded less, on average, than will more casual customers and tourists.

Darby and Karni conclude their paper by discussing market arrangements which may serve to minimize fraudulent practices. One potential arrangement is joint ownership of the durable good and the repair service facility. For example, some users of durable goods may demand sufficient repair services that it becomes cost-effective to maintain their own repair facility. The ability of joint ownership to internalize externalities was discussed in Section 3.1. Another form of joint ownership is to transfer the property rights in the durable good to the repair service facility. Examples of such arrangements are service contracts, warranties, and leases. While these alternative arrangements eliminate repair fraud, they also reduce self-monitoring of care by the user. Thus, leasing-type arrangements merely shift, but do not remove the incentive for opportunism.

A form of informal contract discussed by Darby and Karni is the client relationship in which both parties implicitly understand that the consumer will continue to patronize the repair shop unless he discovers fraud. Long-term client relationships give the consumer an extended time period over which he can discover quality depreciation. Long-term client relationships are, incidentally, characteristic of the exchange of audit services. Finally, Darby and Karni discuss the brand name mechanism as a potential market arrangement to guarantee quality. In their words,

> A firm which, generally, sells honest advice will over time build up a reputation among its clients which enables it to charge a higher price for a given good than competitors whose promises carry less weight. Building up a reputation or satisfied clientele is in the nature of a capital investment, because losses must be borne because of competition of shops with either similar prices and quality and better reputations or similar reputations but lower prices and quality. (p. 82)

Building a reputation is a costly process. Promotional activities such as advertising, free samples, and dissemination of product information consume real resources. Firms may also offer to guarantee product quality ("your money back if not completely satisfied") and they may advertise an image of long term stability, such as Maytag. Mercedes, for example, advertises that it changes body styles less often than do other automobile manufacturers. One method used by auditing firms which "keeps their name before the public" is to distribute information on current accounting issues which may be of interest to clients (and other individuals). For example, Ernst and Whinney publishes an International Series about tax, accounting, and other government requirements in various countries, as well as a series entitled Financial Reporting Developments. Another method used specifically by public accounting firms is to support auditing and accounting research. For example, over the time period 1976-1980, the Peat, Marwick, Mitchell Foundation is devoting $2,000,000 to its Research Opportunities in Auditing program.

The capital investments acquired to build a reputation should satisfy several criteria. First, they should be firm-specific, that is, readily identifiable by consumers as attaching to a particular firm. For example, accounting information which is disseminated by auditing firms should carry the name of the auditing firm. Second, these investments should be readily observable to consumers. If possible, they should also be sunk costs to the firm, in the sense that they are virtually useless, should this particular firm depreciate the quality of its product. In this manner, these capital investments can serve as collateral, i.e., provide the firm with "something to lose" if it depreciates product quality. Finally, if possible, these capital expenditures should be beneficial to consumers and/or other individuals. For example, the accounting publications and research sponsored by public accounting firms are beneficial to clients (and to auditing researchers) as well as to the public accounting firms themselves.

All of the activities enumerated above consume real resources. Therefore, as Barzel [1979] notes, the brand name mechanism is a costly process, as are the other alternative arrangements which Darby and Karni discuss. But, in at least some cases, these alternative arrangements are less costly than the cost to consumers of producer deception, because we do observe them in the marketplace. Again, if it is costly to discover quality depreciation, brand naming will minimize, but not remove all fraud.

A model of costly quality determination in which a brand name arrangement is sufficient to remove all fraud is provided by Klein and Leffler [forthcoming]. In the Klein and Leffler model, goods are either high or low quality goods. It is prohibitively costly for consumers to observe quality pre-purchase, although they are assumed to know which firm produced the goods and the cost functions of firms. Fraud occurs when producers deceptively sell the low quality goods at the high quality price. Producers are able to "cheat" only once because consumers will discover the fraud post-purchase and will immediately (and costlessly) terminate the firm. Thus a firm which depreciates quality will experience a one-time gain and then lose all future business.

Klein and Leffler assert that one mechanism which will guarantee the supply of the high quality good is a "quality guaranteeing price." This price is a premium paid for quality sufficient to ensure that the present value of the future premium stream exceeds the one-time gain from depreciating quality. Consumers are willing to pay a price premium above the perfectly competitive (costless information about quality) price in order to guarantee quality. Competition among producers will ensure that the quality guaranteeing price will be the lowest possible, i.e., the price for high quality at which producers will be just indifferent between cheating and not cheating. Competition among producers, however, cannot drive the equilibrium price below the quality guaranteeing price or "cheating" will occur. Therefore, in a non-deceptive equilibrium, any profits will be competed away on non-price dimensions. Klein and Leffler's model suggests that this non-price competition takes the form of firm-specific investment in brand name capital.

A producer's investment in brand name capital must meet two criteria in order to serve as a type of collateral bond to deter quality depreciation. First, it must be firm-specific so that its value is tied in to the firm. Second, it must have an essentially zero salvage value, i.e., its value in other uses must be very low. These two characteristics enable the investment in brand name capital to guarantee quality because it gives the firm "something to lose" should it depreciate quality. In equilibrium, producers will invest in brand name capital until they just earn a normal rate of return on these assets. In a Klein and Leffler equilibrium, no fraud will occur because

(1) Consumers know producers' cost functions and thus are able to costlessly determine the quality guaranteeing price, and

(2) Consumers are assumed to instantly and costlessly terminate producers who "cheat."

In the absence of an information asymmetry between producers and consumers, the equilibrium amount of fraud will be zero. While this result is descriptively unappealing, the Klein and Leffler model is useful in understanding how quality-guaranteeing mechanisms are likely to operate.

To summarize this section: we first reviewed three papers in the auditing literature which discuss auditor brand naming and its potential importance in the exchange of audit services. None of these papers attempts to analyze the mechanisms by which auditor brand name may serve to guarantee quality where quality determination is costly. In order to examine this process more closely, we reviewed two models of costly quality determination from the economics literature.

In the following chapter, we consider the attribute which enables an auditor's opinion to have value to clients, the independence of the auditor from the client, and we explore the interaction between auditor independence and the equilibrium pricing of audit services.

4

Auditor Independence and the Intertemporal Pricing of Audit Services

In this chapter we examine the link between auditor independence and the fee structure of audit services. Regulators and the accounting profession have asserted that bidding below total cost on initial audit engagements ("low balling") impairs auditor independence. We analyze this assertion by first discussing the economic benefits of auditor independence in Section 4.1. The existence of potential benefits to independence provides auditors and clients with the incentive to contract in a manner which enables both parties to capture these benefits. In Section 4.2, we discuss some aspects of the audit process and the market for audit services which impair auditor independence by creating a material financial interest in the client as an ongoing business entity. Specifically, these attributes are the presence of potential learning-by-doing advantages (a technological parameter) and positive transactions costs of changing auditors. In Section 4.3, we document current regulatory and professional concern about the effects of "low balling" on auditor independence. In Section 4.4., a simple two period model of the auditor's fee choice in the presence of learning-by-doing advantages and transactions costs of changing auditors is presented. This model generates testable implications about the equilibrium pricing of audit services. These hypotheses are formally stated in Section 4.5, where we conclude the chapter by discussing the implications of the model for the current regulatory environment.

4.1 The Economic Benefits of Auditor Independence

In the audit process, the auditor transforms client-prepared data into audited financial statements by accumulating sufficient evidence to enable him to issue an opinion on them. In this process, the auditor adds value to the financial statements by utilizing his professional skills and assets, which include technical and investigative skills, any specialized knowledge of client operations, and his professional reputation for independence and integrity. In order for his opinion to have value in the capital market, the auditor must have some incentive to tell the "truth" when the truth is "bad news" from the client's perspective.[1] In fact, the auditor's incentive to reveal "bad news" when it is not in the client's narrow self interest to do so can be viewed as a definition of auditor independence. As stated in the Cohen Report,

> ... the obligations created by the audit function may require the auditor to persuade management to present a measurement of earnings or disclose material information that reflects unfavorably on its performance. Often, the independent auditor's task is to persuade people to do precisely what they do not want to do. (p. 105)

Thus, the value of an audit to consumers of audit services may depend on the auditor's ability to withstand client pressures to disclose selectively.

If the auditor's incentives were perfectly aligned with his client's narrow self interest, then the auditor may not have the incentive to reveal the "truth" in certain states of the world. For example, an auditor may have the incentive to attest falsely to the financial statements of a financially troubled client because the continuation of the client allows the auditor to capture positive economic profits in future periods. The closer the perceived alignment of incentives between the auditor and the client, the lower the value of the auditor's opinion of the client's financial statements to consumers of audit services. In an efficient capital market, the expected economic benefits of auditor independence will be fully reflected in the client's share price.

Rather than attempt a definition of auditor independence, the accounting profession and regulators have operationalized the concept by delineating those situations in which auditor independence is likely to be impaired. Both the SEC and the AICPA agree that auditor independence is presumed to be impaired if the auditor possesses a material financial interest in the continuation of the client as a business entity. We shall refer to this concept of auditor independence as the "economic interest" concept. The "economic interest" concept presumes that the auditor is not independent with respect to a client in which he possesses a material economic interest. In fact, "economic interest" is a necessary, but not sufficient, condition for auditor opportunism to occur. An economic interest in the client sets up the incentive for misrepresentation; in order for "cheating" to actually occur, it is also necessary that auditors perceive the marginal benefits from misrepresentation to exceed the marginal costs.[2]

In an efficient capital market, rational agents will forecast that auditors who possess a known economic interest in their clients have increased incentives for opportunism, and these incentives will be reflected in the client's share price. Since perceived auditor independence has potential economic benefits to clients (through its impact on firm value) and to auditors (through the fees they are able to charge for audit services), we would expect the parties to voluntarily choose contractual arrangements which enable them to capture these benefits. That is, absent regulation, clients have the incentive to contract with auditors in such a way as to maximize the incremental firm value from auditing. Efficient capital markets and competition in the market for audit services will govern the extent to which auditor independence will be impaired by the actions of rational clients and auditors.

4.2 The Existence of Specialized Assets Creates Future Economic Interest

There are, however, certain technological parameters in the production of audit services which serve to impair auditor independence in the "economic interest" sense. One of these parameters is the existence of comparative cost advantages to an incumbent auditor at the recontracting interval, due to significant learning-by-doing advantages in the provision of audit services.

It is well recognized in the literature that initial audit engagements entail significant start-up costs. Arens and Loebbecke [1976] provide three reasons for this phenomenon:

(1) It is necessary to verify the details making up those balance sheet accounts that are of a permanent nature, such as fixed assets, patents, and retained earnings.

(2) It is necessary to verify the beginning balances in the balance sheet accounts on an initial engagement.

(3) The auditor is less familiar with the client's operations in an initial audit. (p. 100)

The presence of fixed start-up costs on initial audit engagements implies that a material learning-by-doing aspect is present with audit services. We call this learning-by-doing aspect the existence of specialized assets between a given auditor-client pair. Learning-by-doing advantages are an asset because they provide future economic benefits to auditors and clients. These assets are specialized because they relate to a particular auditor and a particular client. Since these assets are specialized to both parties, we would expect the incentives associated with the existence of specialized assets to be bilateral. For example, both the client and the auditor have incentives to maintain a relationship, once established.

The importance of specialized assets to auditor-client contracting is that they provide incumbent auditors with a comparative cost advantage over competitors in subsequent audits of a given client. Once an auditor has performed an initial audit for a given client, he has acquired specialized knowledge of that client which enables him to charge a fee for future audits which is greater than his total costs in those periods.[3] This establishes the existence of an "economic interest" in the client which provides the incentive for auditor opportunism, i.e., which impairs auditor independence by the accepted concept.

Competition among auditors, both for the initial audit and at the recontracting interval, will govern the extent to which an incumbent auditor can benefit from learning-by-doing advantages. Competition among auditors will not eliminate the specialized assets problem, because there are no perfect substitutes for the incumbent auditor at the recontracting interval.[4] The existence of specialized assets between a given auditor-client pair results in what Williamson [1975] labels a "small numbers bargaining situation," i.e., a bilateral monopoly.

A numerical example may serve to better illustrate the effect of specialized assets on auditor-client contracting. Assume a two period world in which a particuliar client requires 150 hours of auditor time inputs for the initial audit. If the same auditor is retained for the second period audit, the knowledge gained on the first audit will enable him to perform the second using only 100 hours of auditor time. If a new auditor is engaged for the second period audit, he will be required to input 150 auditor hours. We abstract from last period problems (see Chapter 3) by assuming that contracts are perfectly enforceable in the second period.

The competitive hourly price for auditors, which are assumed to be initially identical and therefore perfect substitutes for each other, is $50 per hour. The client will solicit bids, and competition among auditors in first round negotiations will ensure a competitive solution. If it were the case that the auditor's $2,500 investment ($50 x 50 hours) in learning the client's operations had zero value to him in the future, he would force the client to make the investment, i.e., to pay the auditor $7,500 the first year and $5,000 thereafter. But this is clearly not the case. In future years, the incumbent auditor can charge this particular client an audit fee greater than $5,000. The amount by which his future audit fee exceeds $5,000 depends on the relative bargaining power of auditor and client and the transactions costs of switching auditors (assumed to be zero in this example). In addition, competition among auditors in the second period limits the fees which an incumbent auditor can charge in that period to an amount less than or equal to the alternative supply price at that time. By terminating the client, the auditor can impose costs of $2,500 on the client (to train a new auditor). If he has any bargaining power at all vis à vis the client, he will be able to extract audit fees of up to $2,500 over his costs in the second period. Therefore, the auditor's investment in specialized knowledge has future economic benefit to him; he would be willing to incur some of the $2,500 start-up fees, i.e., to bill the client below total cost on the initial audit engagement with the expectation of higher (than current total costs) audit fees in the second period.

The important point of this example is that, no matter which party absorbs the initial start-up costs, their existence creates an "economic interest" in the client on the part of the incumbent auditor. "Low-balling" by the initial auditor is a competitive response to the existence of future "economic interest;" "low-balling" itself does not cause future profits to be greater than zero. Because the incumbent auditor can capture a higher (than current total costs) audit fee next period, he has some incentive to misrepresent a troubled client's financial status in the current period. And the greater the future economic interest, the greater the incentive to falsely attest in order to retain a given client.

If contracting between auditors and clients were costless, the parties would contract at time zero to remove the bilateral monopoly (and associated independence) problems at time one. The incentive to do so is certainly present, because both parties will benefit if the capital market views them as totally independent from each other. However, when contracting among individuals is costly, it will generally not be optimal to reduce to zero the probability that the auditor sets audit fees at time one above total costs at that time. And as long as some potential for positive future economic profit remains, auditor independence is impaired by the "economic interest" concept.

Specialized assets are not only specific to the auditor; they are specific to the client as well. We have seen that the auditor can impose costs on the client by terminating him and forcing him to train a new auditor. The client can also impose costs on the auditor by terminating him and forcing him to lose the present value of future economic profit due to his specialized knowledge of this client. This is the case because the auditor's specialized knowledge is, by assumption, useful only on audits of this client. The non-marketability of the auditor's specialized knowledge prevents him from capturing a return on it, should the client terminate him. Were this asset marketable to other auditors,[5] the client's threat to terminate the auditor would carry less economic impact. Since this specialized knowledge is not marketable, the client is able to impose material costs on the auditor by terminating him. Auditors will take this possibility into account when bidding on initial audit engagements. So while initial engagements may be negotiated in a competitive environment, once this audit is completed and a specialized asset is created, auditors and clients are locked into a small numbers bargaining situation, i.e., a bilateral monopoly. Auditors' and clients' rational expectations ex ante will recognize this future condition, and these expectations will be reflected in the sharing fraction applied to the $2,500 start-up costs. In general, the solution will not be a corner one; competition among auditors in first round negotiations will ensure that the rate of return expected on the investment in specialized assets (including negotiation costs) will be a normal one.

The numerical example illustrates that "low-balling," i.e., bidding below total costs in the first period, is a competitive response to the specialized asset-induced expectation of higher (than current total costs) audit fees in future periods. The existence of specialized assets also provides the joint incentive to continue an auditor-client relationship, once established, i.e., both auditor and client tend to "lose" in economic terms if an established relationship is terminated.

Another factor in the exchange of audit services which provides auditors with "economic interest" in their clients is the presence of positive transactions costs of changing auditors. By terminating a client, auditors can impose these transactions costs on the client. Therefore, if auditors possess any bargaining power vis à vis the client, they can capture at least part of these costs by raising audit fees in future periods. Thus, positive transactions costs of changing auditors also provide auditors with an "economic interest" in their clients, and therefore impair auditor independence by the accepted concept. An analogous argument to that presented above for the specialized asset case would show that "low-balling" and long-term auditor-client relationships are a rational response to the existence of positive costs of changing auditors.

4.3 Current Regulatory Interest

We have seen that the existence of specialized assets (a technological parameter) and exogenously-imposed transactions costs of switching auditors leads to at least two responses:

(1) Competition among auditors will force auditors to "low-ball," i.e., to bid below cost on initial audit engagements, and

(2) Clients and auditors have the incentive to continue an established relationship.

Both of these responses are endogenously determined, and will vary in response to a change in an underlying parameter. Neither of these responses is a cause of impaired independence.

The accounting profession and the SEC, however, have traditionally asserted that (1) and (2) themselves cause impaired independence. Mandatory auditor rotation has been an issue for many years. "Low-balling" has recently come under attack as well. For example, the Commission on Auditor's Responsibilities (the Cohen Commission) was charged in 1974 by the American Institute of Certified Public Accountants to "develop conclusions and recommendations regarding the appropriate responsibilities of independent auditors." The Commission Report, issued in 1978, contends that

There are allegations, however, that firms sometimes offer relatively low fees for the first year or the first few years on an audit, with the expectation of recovering the initial loss in subsequent years.

An ethics ruling of the AICPA indicates that when the preceding year's audit fee remains unpaid, independence is impaired: this prohibition is based on the belief that such a receivable from the client gives the auditor an interest in the financial success of the client and might influence his independence in carrying out the examination.

We believe that accepting an audit engagement with the expectation of offsetting early losses or lower revenues with fees to be charged in future audits creates the same condition and represents the same threat to independence. (p. 121). (emphasis added)

The Securities and Exchange Commission, partly in response to the Cohen Commission Report, issued Securities Act Release No. 33-5869 in September, 1977. According to this release,

The Commission is also concerned about the possible effect on the auditor's independence and objectivity of an understanding or agreement limiting the auditor's fee to an absolute amount. Accordingly, the proposed rule would require disclosure of any such agreement.

The final rule, ASR-250, which became effective for proxy statements subsequent to September 30, 1978 reads,

Describe any existing direct or indirect understanding or agreement that places a limit on current or future years' audit fees, including fee arrangements that provide fixed limits on fees that are not subject to reconsideration if unexpected issues involving accounting or auditing are encountered.

Thus, the issue of how "low-balling" affects auditor independence is an important one at this time both to the accounting profession and to the SEC. In order to further explore this issue, we provide a formal model of audit pricing in the following section. This model generates testable implications about the effect of changes in transaction costs and in learning-by-doing advantages on the equilibrium pricing of audit services.

4.4 A Two-Period Model of Audit Pricing

In this section, we develop a two-period model of audit pricing which explicitly recognizes the existence of specialized assets and positive transactions costs of changing auditors. The "low-balling" phenomenon is modeled as a competitive response to differences in the two parameters of interest (learning-by-doing and costs of switching auditors). The theory predicts that, ceteris paribus, "low-balling" will increase as a response to increases in either parameter. We formulate these hypotheses in testable form in Section 4.5, in which we also discuss the implications for extant regulation governing audit fees and changes of auditor.

In order to concentrate on pricing effects and to simplify the analysis, we characterize the audit process by auditor inputs and outputs only and ignore client inputs.[6] The output of the audit process is the auditor's opinion on client-prepared financial statements. In this formulation, audit output is vector-valued, consisting of a given auditor's stated opinion with an associated quality dimension, i.e., the degree of confidence which users of audit services place in that opinion. The quality of a given auditor's opinion is evaluated in the capital market, and depends on the capital market's assessment of the auditor's incentives to attest falsely. In this formulation, audit quality is a function of auditor-client contractual attributes: the existence of learning-by-doing advantages, positive transactions costs of changing auditors, and the relative bargaining power of the two parties to the contract. In other words, the form of the contract between auditor and client sets up certain incentives for the parties' behavior, which in turn affects the quality of the output of the audit process (as evaluated by consumers of audit services).

In this chapter, the quality of audit services is assumed to be exogenous and fixed, in order to isolate the "low-balling" phenomenon. In the following chapter, however, the quality dimension of audit output is endogenously determined as a function of the contractual attributes. Specifically, the quality dimension of audit services is modeled in the next chapter as the impact on client firm value of retaining the original auditor for future audits. In the current chapter, the quality of audit services is assumed to be fixed.

We employ a two date model ($t=0,1$) where auditor inputs supplied at time zero are a technological parameter, i.e., A_0 = auditor input at time zero, is fixed and is the same for all potential auditors. Except for learning-by-doing advantages and positive transactions costs of changing auditors, the market for audit services is assumed to be competitive throughout. In the current model, audit output is assumed to be fixed and identical over both time periods and across all potential auditors. Audit output is fixed on initial audits by the assumption that, given a fixed level of auditor inputs, A_0, all (identical) auditors agree on the client's financial status. With both auditor input and output held constant, a unique audit output point is determined for the firm, by assumption. The value of a given auditor's opinion is set in the capital market and is the subject of the following chapter.

If a new (i.e., not the incumbent) auditor audits the client at time one, he is presumed to face an identical production function for audit services at that time. In other words, the conditions faced on initial audit engagements are identical for all auditors, regardless of whether the engagement takes place at time zero or at time one. Therefore, A_0 is auditor input on all initial audit engagements. In addition, the total audit fees charged by first time auditors at time zero only are defined to be fee$_0$. Because time one in this model is the last period,[7] first time auditors at time one will set audit fees equal to total costs at that time. Defining w as the per unit opportunity cost of auditors (assumed to be the same for all auditors over both time periods), audit fees for new auditors at time one will equal wA_0.

In addition, we define the following terms:

- r = The discount rate, which is parametric and identical for all auditors and clients over both time periods.
- π_0, π_1 = The auditor's profit (total revenues minus total costs) at $t=0$ and $t=1$, respectively.
- C = The transactions cost of changing auditors, assumed to be a fixed constant. These costs may include search costs of finding a new auditor, the costs of complying with regulation which mandates disclosure of the circumstances surrounding a change of auditors, etc.

Some portion of A_0, call it α, indexes learning-by-doing (the higher α, the more learning-by-doing).[8] The effect of the alpha parameter is to give the incumbent auditor a comparative cost advantage over competitors in the second ($t=1$) round. The incumbent auditor's production function for audit services at time one is a function both of auditor inputs at $t=1$ and of αA_0, what was learned from auditing that particular client at $t=0$. Specifically, define the incumbent auditor's inputs at $t=1$ to be equal to

$$A_1 = (1 - \alpha)A_0$$

The value of specialized assets to the incumbent auditor is that they enable him to supply this client's time one audit services at lower cost than potential competitors. The alternative suppliers of audit services at $t = 1$ must provide auditor inputs equal to A_0 to audit this client, where $A_0 > A_1 = (1 - \alpha)A_0$. The total audit fee which the incumbent auditor charges at time one, given that he audited the client at time zero, is defined to be fee$_1$. With costly contracting, the existence of learning-by-doing ($\alpha > 0$) and positive transactions costs of changing auditors ($C > 0$) implies a bilateral monopoly between client and incumbent auditor at time one. The solution (equilibrium price) depends on the relative bargaining power of the two parties. We can, however, characterize the range in which the solution will lie.

The total revenues to the incumbent auditor at time one will lie in the range $(wA_1, wA_0 + C)$. The incumbent auditor's costs at time one, wA_1, provide a lower bound on total revenues at that time. He will be unwilling to perform the audit for less than his total costs. The maximum amount the incumbent auditor can charge at $t=1$ is the cost to the client of having the audit performed by a new auditor plus the transactions costs of changing auditors. Since time one in this model is the last period, a new auditor will set total revenues equal to total costs, wA_0. The existence of potential learning-by-doing advantages at time one is of no economic consequence to new auditors at that time because $t=1$ is the last period. A positive alpha has value to an auditor only if it enables him to enjoy a comparative cost advantage over competitors in future periods. The total revenues which the incumbent auditor can charge at time one are limited by the threat of competition to be less than or equal to the alternative supply price plus the cost of changing auditors:

$$\text{fee}_1 \leq wA_0 + C$$

In order to make "relative bargaining power" explicit in the model, we introduce the parameter θ, which represents the share of the time one premium which the incumbent auditor can capture. We define the auditor's profit at time one to be

$$\pi_1 = \text{fee}_1 - wA_1 = \theta(wA_0 + C - wA_1)$$
$$= \theta(C + \alpha wA_0) \text{ where } 0 < \theta \leq 1$$

In this model, it must be the case that θ is strictly greater than zero because contracting is assumed to be costly. Costless contracting would enable the parties to drive θ to zero, the incumbent auditor would be unable to capture any learning-by-doing advantages at time one, and the problem would reduce to the competitive case. By assuming that contracting between auditor and client is costly, we are implicitly assuming that $\theta > 0$. Also, competition among auditors at time one assures that $\theta \leq 1$. In the current model, where audit output is identical for all auditors, clients will be indifferent between retaining and terminating the incumbent auditor when $\theta = 1$. This statement does not continue to hold in the following chapter, when audit output is allowed to vary across auditors.

The use of a two period model, while admittedly a simplification, highlights the "low-balling" phenomenon without unduly complicating the analysis. In a multiperiod model, the existence of specialized assets enables the original auditor to charge a higher (than total costs) audit fee in every future period. The extent to which the incumbent auditor can raise future fees, however, is limited; with zero transactions costs of switching auditors, the present value of the incumbent auditor's total fees cannot exceed the present value of the total cost to the client of training two auditors. Assuming noncollusive behavior, these two auditors will be perfect competitors in every future period. In other words, in the absence of prohibitive transactions costs of changing auditors, the strategy of training two non-colluding auditors would completely remove the bilateral monopoly problem in all future periods.[9] Thus, this strategy places an upper bound on the amount an incumbent auditor can charge the client for future audit engagements. The qualitative predictions of the multiperiod model are unchanged from the implications of the simple two date model formulated in this section.[10]

Uncertainty can be incorporated in the analysis by making the auditor's future economic profit probabilistic. The economic profit which the incumbent auditor can capture at time one is dependent on being retained by this particular client at that time. As mentioned earlier, the non-marketability of the auditor's specialized knowledge of clients implies a salvage value of essentially zero for specialized assets. The auditor's expected future fee, therefore, depends on his assessment of the probability of retention by the client. Define ϕ_R as the probability that the client will retain the incumbent auditor at time one. Then the auditor's expected economic profit at time one is

$$E(\pi_1) = \phi_R \theta [C + \alpha w A_0]$$

In order to concentrate on this expected future economic profit without considering its variance, we add the additional assumption that auditors and clients are risk neutral.

The probability of retaining the incumbent auditor at time one depends on the opportunity cost to the client of not retaining him, i.e., depends on the cost to the client of changing auditors at that time. This cost, in turn, depends on

(1) the transactions cost of changing auditors, C, and
(2) the amount by which a new auditor's costs exceed the incumbent auditor's costs, which is a function of learning advantages, i.e., of α.

We can write this functional dependence as

$$\phi_R = \phi_R(C, \alpha)$$

As the costs (both technological and transactions) of changing auditors increase, firms are less likely to change auditors, audit quality constant.[11] Therefore,

$$\frac{\partial \phi_R}{\partial C} > 0 \text{ and } \frac{\partial \phi_R}{\partial \alpha} > 0$$

We assert that the auditor maximizes his expected profit, $E(\pi)$, which equals his (certain) profit at time $t=0$ plus the discounted value of his expected profit at $t=1$:

$$\underset{\text{fee}_0}{\text{maximize}} \; E(\pi) = \pi_0 + \frac{E(\pi_1)}{(1+r)}$$

$$= \text{fee}_0 - wA_0 + \frac{\phi_R \theta [C + \alpha w A_0]}{(1+r)} \tag{1}$$

Competition among auditors will ensure that the zero profit condition obtains overall, i.e.,

$$E(\pi^*) = \pi_0^* + \frac{E(\pi_1^*)}{(1+r)} = 0$$

where asterisks denote equilibrium values.[12] With positive values of α, C, and θ, i.e., in the presence of potential learning-by-doing advantages, transactions costs of switching auditors, and the ability to make credible threats, a positive profit will be earned at time one.[13] The equilibrium audit fee at time zero, fee_0^*, is that fee which satisfies the zero profit condition that

$$E(\pi^*) = \text{fee}_0^* - wA_0 + \frac{\phi_R \theta [C + \alpha w A_0]}{(1+r)} = 0 \tag{2}$$

Since $E(\pi_1^*)$, the expected time one economic profit, is positive, π_0^*, the time zero profit, must be negative in order that the zero profit condition be met over both time periods. Therefore, we can infer that

$$\text{fee}_0^* < wA_0$$

which establishes the presence of "low-balling" in the initial period.

While the initial period audit fee, fee_0^*, is modeled here as a choice variable, in actuality fee_0^* is determined by the interaction of supply and demand in the marketplace. In a general equilibrium framework with zero information costs regarding prices, auditors who set their initial fees greater than fee_0^* will attract no clients. Similarly, if an auditor were to set fees below fee_0^*, all clients would patronize that auditor, quality constant. However, at $\text{fee}_0 < \text{fee}_0^*$, negative profits will be earned over both time periods combined, and no auditor would be able to sustain this pricing policy. Therefore, in a general equilibrium setting, competition among auditors will ensure that all (identical) auditors set initial audit fees equal to fee_0^*.

Additional insights can be gained from the model by comparing the equilibrium price of audit services, fee_0^*, derived in (2) to the perfectly competitive (with zero fixed costs) price, fee_0^c. Since, under perfect competition, zero profits are earned in each period, the equilibrium value of fee_0^c is the one which satisfies

$$\text{fee}_0^c - wA_0 = 0 \tag{3}$$

Equating (2) and (3) yields

$$\text{fee}_0^c - \text{fee}_0^* = \frac{\phi_R \theta [C + \alpha w A_0]}{(1+r)} \tag{4}$$

which says that, for positive values of θ, α, and C, the auditor will choose $\text{fee}_0^* < \text{fee}_0^c$ by that amount which enables him to earn an expected normal rate of return on the investment in specialized assets.

Solving equation (2) for fee_0^*, the equilibrium audit fee at time zero, yields

$$\text{fee}_0^* = wA_0 - \frac{\phi_R \theta [C + \alpha w A_0]}{(1+r)} \tag{5}$$

The structure of the model can be easily seen by differentiating (5) with respect to θ to get

$$\frac{\partial \text{fee}_0^*}{\partial \theta} = -\frac{\phi_R [C + \alpha w A_0]}{(1+r)} < 0 \tag{6}$$

which says that the effect of an increase in θ is to lower $t=0$ audit fees by exactly the present value of the amount by which future audit fees are expected to increase for an increase in θ. Thus, the present value of the effect on future audit fees of changes in θ is exactly offset by a change in current fees. This offsetting effect is a direct implication of the auditor's zero profit condition at equilibrium, as well as the independence of ϕ_R from θ. The model is extreme in the sense that all expected cost savings of retaining the incumbent auditor for both periods accrue to clients. This result is an implication of competition among auditors.[14]

The comparative statics implications of the model are obtained by differentiating equation (5) with respect to the parameters of interest, in this case C and α. First, differentiating with respect to C yields

$$\frac{\partial \text{fee}_0^*}{\partial C} = -\frac{\theta}{(1+r)} [\phi_R + \frac{\partial \phi_R}{\partial C} (C + \alpha w A_0)] < 0 \qquad (7)$$

which says that, as the costs of changing auditors increase, there are greater expected benefits for the auditor to capture at time one, and thus he will be increasingly willing to "low-ball" at time zero.

We can also analyze how a change in the alpha parameter will induce a change in the time zero audit fee. Differentiating (5) with respect to alpha yields

$$\frac{\partial \text{fee}_0^*}{\partial \alpha} = -\frac{\theta}{(1+r)} [\phi_R w A_0 + \frac{\partial \phi_R}{\partial \alpha} (C + \alpha w A_0)] < 0 \qquad (8)$$

As learning-by-doing advantages increase for clients, the auditor who expects to be retained in the following period will be increasingly willing to lower his time zero fee.

In summary, our model explicitly recognizes the alleged "low-balling" phenomenon which is of current concern to regulators and to the accounting profession. Defining "low-balling" as a lower than perfectly competitive (with no fixed costs) price at $t=0$, the model predicts that increased "low-balling" by auditors is a response to

(1) Increased learning-by-doing advantages, and/or

(2) Increased transactions costs of changing auditors.

4.5 Testable Implications and Current Regulation

Recent SEC regulation has increased the transactions costs of changing auditors by requiring increased disclosure of the circumstances surrounding the change. Four rules are relevant: Securities Exchange Act Release No. 34-9344 (effective October 31, 1971), ASR-165 (effective January 1, 1975), ASR-194 (effective August 31, 1976), and ASR-247 (effective July 31, 1978). The main provisions of these rules are described in Appendix C. The stated purpose of the regulation was to strengthen auditor independence by increasing auditors' ability to withstand client pressures. For example, in its discussion in ASR-165, the SEC states that "This (Securities Release No. 34-9344) was designed to strengthen accountants' independence by discouraging the practice of changing accountants in order to obtain more favorable accounting treatment."

The Cohen Report supports the SEC position on auditor changes, and the asserted impact of the regulation on auditor independence. In fact, the Cohen Commission recommends that disclosure of auditor changes comparable to that required by ASR-165 should be included in management's report in the firm's financial statements. According to the Cohen Report, "measures that increase the outside scrutiny of a change in independent auditors are likely to inhibit the tendency to apply pressure to the independent auditor by threatening dismissal" (p. 107).

Neither the SEC nor the Cohen Commission recognized the bilateral monopoly situation between incumbent auditor and client. In a bilateral monopoly, to increase the costs of changing auditors is to raise the future audit fees which the incumbent auditor can charge. Higher future audit fees impair auditor independence by the "economic interest" concept. Thus, SEC regulation, while it may have strengthened the auditor's ability to withstand client pressures, may also have weakened auditor independence by the accepted concept. Two effects are present here, only one of which was previously recognized by the SEC and the accounting profession. On the one hand, ASR-165 et al. may have strengthened auditor independence by enabling auditors to better withstand client pressures. On the other hand, because of the bilateral monopoly situation, the regulation may have impaired auditor independence by enabling auditors to raise future audit fees.

In order to compare the relative magnitudes of these two effects, we require a model of the auditor-client relationship which enables one to predict which effect is the stronger of the two. The purpose of Chapter 5 is to provide such a model, or framework within which these questions can be analyzed. Without anticipating the analysis in Chapter 5, we can briefly state the results: whether auditor independence with respect to a given client is increased or decreased by, say, ASR-165, depends on whether the increase in future economic profits from other clients (due to ASR-165) exceeds the increase in future economic profit from this client, due to the regulation. In other words, the future economic profit from other audit clients serves as a collateral bond to restrain auditor opportunism with respect to a particular client. Prior to ASR-165, we can assume that auditors and clients had voluntarily contracted to capture the potential benefits from auditor independence, net of contracting costs. One effect of ASR-165 was to change the costs to the client of terminating the auditor. We can properly conclude that the optimal contractual form subsequent to the regulation will differ from the optimal form prior to the regulation. One function of our formal models is to predict in what direction these changes will occur.

Of the regulation summarized in Appendix C, Securities Release #34-9344 and ASR-165 appear to have the strongest "bite." A testable implication of equation (7) in our model is therefore

H_1: *Ceteris paribus,* the relative incidence of "low-balling," i.e., bidding below total cost on initial audit engagements, has increased in the time period subsequent to Securities Release #34-9344 and ASR-165.

H_1 would be difficult to test because of the difficulty in gathering fee data from auditing firms. The Cohen Commission twice attempted to gather data bearing on the "low-balling" phenomenon, but was unable to acquire sufficient evidence to perform rigorous statistical tests. The extant evidence bearing on H_1 is of an anecdotal nature. For example, the Cohen Report states that

> ... the experiences of some members of the Commission and staff indicate that fee competition is common and *increasing*. (emphasis added)
>
> Discussions with a few companies that have recently negotiated with new auditors indicated readiness on the part of public accounting firms to offer competitive prices, to make bids with fees guaranteed for several years, to renegotiate prices after receipt of competitive offers, and to set billing rates at as much as 50 percent below normal. In a recent article in the Wall Street Journal, the managing partner of a large public accounting firm described the competition in public accounting practice and indicated his own firm's willingness to engage in intense competition. A recently released congressional staff study includes a letter from one practitioner accusing another firm of unfair price competition. (p. 110)

The AICPA publication, *Sample Engagement Letters for an Accounting Practice* [1978], provides a sample of an engagement letter for a new client where the auditor contracts explicitly to absorb first-time costs. The relevant provision from this letter states that

> ... In an initial audit such as this, we must spend a great deal of time getting familiar with your operations, developing the audit program, and learning more about your financial procedures and controls. As we discussed with you, we will absorb such first-time costs as our investment in what we hope will be a continuing relationship with your organziation. (p. 162)

Thus, extant evidence, while anecdotal in nature, is consistent both with the existence and increased incidence of "low-balling."

The difficulty in gathering evidence on price competition should not obscure the importance of economic analysis to this issue. Two points are relevant here. First, the model in this chapter highlights the complexity of the effects of regulation which requires increased disclosure of auditor changes. At the same time that these rules enable the auditor to better withstand client pressures, they also enable him to raise future audit fees (thus creating an increased "economic interest" in this particular client).

Second, these rules are, to some extent, inconsistent with ASR-250, which attempts to curtail "low-balling." For example, ASR-250 states that

> Fee arrangements where the accountant has agreed to a fee significantly less than a fee that would cover expected direct costs in order to obtain the client or in response to criticism of prior services are examples of situations which could require disclosure.

If, as our model predicts, the effect of ASR-165, et. al., is to increase "low-balling," then the result is two layers of costly regulation which are inconsistent with each other (i.e., one layer encourages what the other seeks to discourage). While, in many cases the "costs and benefits" of regulation may be prohibitively costly to measure, in this case one can question the usefulness of two sets of rules which appear to be mutually inconsistent.

Furthermore, our analysis demonstrates that "low-balling" is a response to an underlying parameter which creates "economic interest;" "low-balling" is not the cause of impaired auditor independence. In fact, observation of "low-balling" would suggest that there is some degree of competition in the market for audit services, since "low-balling" is a competitive response to the existence of potential future profits. Our analysis suggests that regulations (or suggestions by the Cohen Commission) which attempt to deal with the issue of auditor independence by curtailing "low-balling" treat the symptom rather than the cause.

Equation (8) from the model provides a second testable implication:

H_2: *Ceteris paribus,* the relative incidence of "low-balling" is greater for those clients for whom potential learning-by-doing advantages are relatively more important.

In order to operationalize this hypothesis, we would need to specify a proxy variable for α, perhaps some measure of the complexity of client operations such as geographic dispersion, number of accounting reports required, etc. Again, both these hypotheses would prove difficult to test because of data availability problems. However, we can introduce another choice variable, the length of the auditor-client contract, which also varies in response to exogenous differences in α and C. In the next chapter, we extend the model to allow variation in the quality dimension of audit output and to incorporate the choice of auditor-client contract length.

5

Specialized Assets, Number of Clients, and Length of the Auditor-Client Relationship

The length of the auditor-client relationship is another variable which can be changed in response to differences in potential learning-by-doing advantages or in the costs of switching auditors. If costless contracting ensured that auditors earned zero profits in every future period, then the length of the auditor-client relationship would be a matter of indifference to auditors (and to clients). Auditors would have no future economic interest in any client, and therefore no direct economic incentive to attest falsely. Costly contracting, learning-by-doing advantages and positive transactions costs of changing auditors creates future economic interest; under these circumstances auditors (and clients) are not indifferent to the length of the auditor-client relationship.

In this chapter, we formulate a two-period model of the client's decision to contract for audit services. Assuming that the decision to contract for an audit has already been made, we examine the choice of the optimal contractual form. Specifically, the decision with which we are concerned in this chapter is whether to contract with one auditor for two time periods (with the associated independence and bilateral monopoly problems at the recontracting interval) or with a new auditor in each period.[1] Intuitively, choosing one auditor for both periods (choosing $T=2$ in our notation) economizes on audit fees. However, as long as the parties cannot contract costlessly over two periods, this strategy also results in "future economic interest" in the client. Choosing $T=1$ (a one period time horizon) avoids the independence problem, but at the cost of a higher present value of audit fees. This chapter's model predicts that the choice of contract is a tradeoff between these two costs: higher audit fees versus the costs of impaired auditor independence.

The chapter is organized as follows: first, in Section 5.1, we discuss the use of explicit and implicit contracts for the exchange of audit services. While explicit contracts between auditors and clients are generally negotiated on an engagement-by-engagement basis, auditor-client relationships are typically long term. The observation of long-standing relationships combined with short term explicit contracts suggests that implicit contracting is an important mechanism in the exchange of audit services. Current regulatory and professional concerns about the length of the auditor-client relationship are discussed in Section 5.1. In Section 5.2., we formulate a model of the auditor's choice of the number of long term audit clients. We also analyze the auditor's incentives to lower audit quality by attesting falsely to the financial statements of a given client. We show that auditor opportunism of this type is constrained by the threat of withdrawal of future business from the auditor's other clients. Intuitively, while the existence of future economic interest in a given client impairs auditor independence with respect to that client, the existence of future economic interest in other clients serves as a collateral bond to guarantee audit quality.

One difference between the Chapter 4 "low-balling" model and the present model is that audit quality is allowed to vary. In Section 5.3, audit quality is modeled as the effect on the client's share price[2] of choosing a given auditor for a pre-specified length of time. The impact of the audit on the client's share price is modeled as a function of the length of the contract and the capital market's assessment of the auditor's incentives to attest falsely (which depends on the contractual attributes). Together, the auditor's and client's decision problems generate six testable implications, which are discussed in Section 5.4. The first three hypotheses are predictions about changes in auditor concentration over time. The second three hypotheses are predictions about cross-sectional and time series variation in the rates at which client firms change auditors. Finally, extant evidence bearing on some of these predictions is examined in Section 5.4.

5.1 Explicit and Implicit Contracting for the Exchange of Audit Services

Both implicit and explicit contractual arrangements are observed for the exchange of audit services. The engagement letter usually serves as the explicit record of the auditor-client contract. These letters are prepared by the auditor and then sent to the client, generally to be returned with the client's signature. Not all auditing firms follow this practice for all engagements, although the use of engagement letters has most likely increased as auditors' legal liability has increased in recent years. Extant empirical evidence on the increased usage of engagement letters to formalize the auditor-client contract is discussed in Appendix D.

One striking characteristic of engagement letters is their short length and relative informality as compared to other business contracts, e.g., bond covenants. Not only are engagement letters relatively informal, but they may not be used at all. And even when they are used to formalize the auditor-client relationship, they are typically issued on an engagement-by-engagement basis, i.e., they cover only a single audit engagement. In other words, the explicit contracts which we observe for the exchange of audit services are generally short term contracts.

There are, however, disadvantages to short term contracts due to the potential for opportunism between the parties. This potential is present because learning-by-doing and transactions costs of changing auditors transform the initial auditor-client relationship into a bilateral monopoly at the recontracting interval. An explanation of how this problem can develop is provided by Williamson [1975]:

(1) Opportunism refers to a lack of candor or honesty in transactions, to include self interest seeking with guile;

(2) Opportunistic inclinations pose little risk as long as competitive (large-numbers) exchange relations obtain;

(3) Many transactions that at the outset involve a large number of qualified bidders are transformed in the process of contract execution, so that a small-numbers supply condition effectively obtains at the contract renewal interval; and

(4) Recurrent short-term contracting is costly and risky when opportunism and transactions of this latter kind are joined. (pp. 9-10)

In spite of the potential problems with short term contracts, if explicit contracts are observed in the exchange of audit services, they are generally short term.

While explicit contracts are generally short term, observed auditor-client relationships are usually of long duration. For example, the Hobgood-Sciarrino [1972] survey of financial executives reported one auditor-client relationship of 50 years duration. This same survey and its follow-up study found that auditor change rates for the firms in their sample were of the order of magnitude of only 3% annually. The empirical observation of long-standing relationships combined with short term explicit contracts suggests that implicit contracting is an important mechanism in the exchange of audit services.

The decision of whether to formalize a relationship by an explicit contract or to rely solely on implicit agreements is an important and interesting one. Macaulay [1963] interviewed businessmen and lawyers in a study of the use of implicit and explicit contracts in business relationships. He defined "contract" as consisting of two distinct elements: rational planning and the availability of legal sanctions to enforce the agreement. Business relationships, according to Macaulay, may be more or less "contractual," depending on the degree to which the parties attempt to delineate all relevant attributes in the written agreement. For example, shareholder-bondholder relationships formalized by bond covenants are typically more "contractual" than are auditor-client relationships.

Macaulay found that businessmen often prefer to rely on implicit agreements, even in the face of exposure to serious risks. Macaulay argues that the parties are more likely to rely on implicit contracts in cases where misunderstandings about product quality or seller performance are less likely to arise. Examples of these cases include the exchange of a standardized product, or a product whose quality can be easily identified pre-purchase. The former case (a standardized product) gives rise to the argument that regulation, by "standardizing" auditor inputs, may economize on contracting costs. The latter case (quality is relatively easy to determine pre-purchase) does not appear to apply to audit services, as argued in Chapter 3 and elsewhere in the auditing literature.

The enforcement of implicit agreements is not generally accomplished by the courts; rather, it relies on the ability of the contracting parties to terminate the agreement if it is not honored. Macaulay cites norms of business behavior which suggest that one should honor contracts. He also points out the critical role played by the thread of withdrawal of future business in enforcing implicit agreements:

> Not only do the particular business units in a given exchange want to deal with each other again, they also want to deal with other business units in the future. And the way one behaves in a particular transaction, or a series of transactions, will color his general business reputation. (p. 64)

While explicit and implicit contracts differ in the availability of legal sanctions to enforce the agreement, both types of contracts rely (at least partially) on the threat of withdrawl of future business as an enforcement mechanism. Since this enforcement mechanism is important to all contracts, it is realistic to analyze contractual relationships in a multiperiod framework.

We have argued that short term contracting poses serious disadvantages in the presence of learning-by-doing and transactions costs of changing auditors. We also argued (in Chapter 4) that the existence of specialized assets and transactions costs provides the bilateral incentive to continue a relationship, once established. Can we therefore conclude that there are no forces which provide auditors and clients with the incentive to terminate an established relationship? The answer is no, for reasons discussed in Chapter 4: that potential benefits from auditor independence provide the incentive for auditors and clients to contract in a manner which enables them to capture these benefits. For example, it is highly unlikely that users would view an auditor as independent from the client if auditor and client were to vertically integrate their operations. In other words, certification by a client's internal audit staff is unlikely to supplant the attest function of the independent auditor.

The choice of either long term contracts or vertical integration as a response to the existence of specialized assets has been analyzed by Klein, Crawford, and Alchian [1978]. Simply put, their argument is that, as the investment in specialized assets increases, the potential for opportunism between the parties also increases, and thus firms are more likely to vertically integrate. In the special case of the market for audit services, the uncertain quality determination of audit services, the information asymmetry between auditor and client about GAAS and GAAP, the existence of specialized assets shared by auditor and client—all would point to vertical integration. However, there are benefits to be gained from auditor independence, as we saw in Chapter 4, and these benefits will preclude explicit vertical integration. Vertical integration can be viewed as a long term contract of infinite length. The presence of learning-by-doing and transactions costs of changing auditors, on the one hand, offset by benefits to auditor-client independence, on the other, is likely to dictate an interior solution.

The length of the auditor-client relationship is a choice variable which can be changed in response to changes in, say, learning-by-doing advantages and transactions costs of changing auditors. A relatively longer relationship does not itself necessarily impair auditor independence. For example, if auditors earned zero economic profits in every period, then increasing the length of the relationship would not increase the present value of the auditor's "future economic interest" in a client. On the other hand, in order for an auditor's "economic interest" in a client to impair auditor independence, the relationship must be expected to continue over future time periods. So while lengthening the relationship does not impair independence per se, it may when coupled with costly contracting. Costly contracting will, in general, prevent the parties from contracting for zero economic profit (to the auditor) in every period. And to the extent that increasing the time horizon increases the present value of future economic profit to the auditor, independence will be impaired by increasing the contract length.

The length of the auditor-client relationship has been of concern to the accounting profession for some time. Recently, the Metcalf Subcommittee has recommended measures to mandate auditor rotation; they assert that the value of a "fresh look" at the client exceeds the costs of changing auditors. The Cohen Commission also studied this issue and recommended that auditor rotation should not be required on the grounds that the technological and transactions costs of rotation are likely to exceed any gains from a "fresh look." In the Commission's view,

> Rotation would considerably increase the cost of audits because of the frequent duplication of the start-up and learning time necessary to gain the familiarity with a company and its operations that is necessary for an effective audit. . . Since the cost of mandatory rotation would be high and the benefits that financial statement users might gain would be

offset by the loss of benefits that result from a continuing relationship, rotation should not be required. (p. 109)

A partial compromise was recently achieved on the issue of auditor rotation; now auditing firms which are members of the SEC practice section must rotate the partner in charge of an audit every five years.[3]

To summarize this section: we discussed the use of explicit versus implicit, and short term versus long term contracts for the exchange of audit services. We characterized the length of the auditor-client relationship as an endogenous response to learning-by-doing advantages and positive transactions costs of changing auditors. While these factors provide auditors and clients with incentives to continue an established relationship, the presence of potential benefits to auditor independence provides a countervailing incentive. Finally, we discussed current regulatory and professional interest in mandatory auditor rotation.

Before characterizing the client's choice of whether to contract with one auditor over both time periods or with a different auditor in each period, we first model the auditor's decision problem. The Chapter 4 "low-balling" model was a one auditor/one client analysis. In the following section, a model is presented which characterizes the auditor's choice of n, the number of long term audit clients. This model highlights the tradeoffs involved in the auditor's decision of whether to attest falsely to the financial statements of a given client. These tradeoffs, in turn, are an input into the client's choice of auditor and contract length, which is formalized in Section 5.3.

5.2 Auditor Size and the Collateral Bond Effect of Specialized Assets

In this section, we show how false attestation is constrained by the threat of withdrawal of future business from an auditor's other clients. If an auditor is assessed as having "cheated" on audit quality, the value of that auditor's opinion to his other current (and potential) clients will decline. For simplicity, we assume that this decline in value to clients is sufficient to cause them to terminate an auditor who is caught lowering audit quality.[4] Furthermore, other quality-guaranteeing arrangements are prohibitively costly to enforce. In this framework, an auditor's future economic profit from other clients serves as a collateral bond to guarantee the audit quality supplied to a particular client. The analysis is admittedly incomplete because we analyze the audit quality supplied to a particular client while holding audit quality on all other clients fixed. However, the appropriateness of the simplifying assumptions of the model ultimately rests on the empirical validity of the model's predictions (see Chapter 5, note 1).

The order of presentation is as follows: we first formulate the auditor's choice of n, the number of two period audit clients. On the surface, this model appears quite similar to an *n*-client formulation of the "low-balling" model from Chapter 4. However, the current model differs from the Chapter 4 model in two respects. First, the auditor's choice variable in the "low-balling" model was the time zero audit fee, fee$_0$. Here, fee$_0$ is modeled as a function of the number of $T=2$ time horizon clients chosen by the auditor,[5] i.e.,

$$\text{fee}_0 = \text{fee}_0(n)$$

where *n* is the auditor's choice variable. In both the "low-balling" and the current model, however, the equilibrium audit fees are determined by the interaction of supply and demand in the market for audit services.

A second difference between the current model and the Chapter 4 "low-balling" model is that auditors are no longer assumed to be identical. Specifically, auditors can differ from each other in only one respect; the ability to manage a large number of two period audit clients. Some auditors may possess a comparative advantage in coordinating a number of audit clients. Defining $c^i(n)$ as the cost of coordinating *n* two period clients to auditor *i*, $c^i(n)$ will in general differ across auditors.[6] We also assume that $c^i(n)$ is increasing in *n* such that $c_n^i > 0, c_{nn}^i > 0$, where c_n^i is the first derivative of $c^i(n)$ with respect to *n* and c_{nn}^i is the second derivative of $c^i(n)$ with respect to *n*. Introducing coordination costs of this general form allows us to summarize conveniently those auditor attributes which lead some auditors to acquire a large number of audit clients, while other auditors do not. Because auditors vary in the ability to coordinate their long term audit clients, auditors of various sizes (i.e., with differing optimal n^*) will exist at equilibrium.

The comparative statics results of the auditor's choice problem generate several testable implications about auditor concentration in the market for audit services. Before modeling the client's choice problem in Section 5.3, we characterize the probability that an auditor who has chosen $n=n^*$ will attest falsely to the financial statements of a given client. This probability is shown to depend on the number of long term audit clients chosen by the auditor. The analysis serves to highlight the collateral bond nature of the future economic profit from an auditor's other audit clients. It also serves to characterize how the auditor's incentives for false attestation change as the number of his two period audit clients changes. The capital market's assessment of the auditor's incentives is an important input into the client's choice of contract length, which is the subject of Section 5.3.

The current model, like the Chapter 4 model, is a two period one, where $t=0$ is the first period and $t=1$ is the second period. Clients are assumed to maximize firm value by choosing an auditor who is characterized by having *n* audit clients. Auditors are asserted to maximize expected profits by choosing *n*, the total number of two period horizon clients.[7] Clients are assumed to be

58   The Auditor-Client Relationship

identical. Auditors are assumed to possess identical w, A_0, C, r, and α, where these variables are defined in Chapter 4. For convenience, the definitions are repeated below:

A_0 = auditor input on initial audit engagements.

α indexes learning-by-doing, where $0 < \alpha \leq 1$

A_1 = time one auditor inputs, given the auditor is incumbent, where $A_1 = (1 - \alpha)A_0 < A_0$

$\text{fee}_0(n)$ = the total audit fee at time zero

fee_1 = $\theta(C + \alpha w A_0) + w A_1$ = the total audit fee of the incumbent auditor at time one where

θ = the relative bargaining power of the auditor with respect to the client, and $0 < \theta \leq 1$.

w = the per unit opportunity cost of auditors, assumed to be the same for all auditors over both time periods.

r = the discount rate, which is parametric and identical for all auditors and clients over both time periods.

π_0, π_1 = the auditor's profit (total revenues minus total costs) at $t=0$ and $t=1$, respectively.

C = the transactions cost of changing auditors, assumed to be a fixed constant. These costs may include the search costs of finding a new auditor, the costs of complying with regulation which mandates disclosure of the circumstances surrounding a change of auditors, etc.

$\phi_R(n)$ = the probability that the auditor will be retained by the client for the time one audit. ϕ_R is a function of n because, as shown later in this section, the probability of auditor opportunism decreases in n.

In addition, as in Chapter 4, auditors and clients are assumed to be risk neutral. Finally, auditor brand name and other quality-guaranteeing arrangements are assumed to be prohibitively costly.

Some additional comments about $\phi_R(n)$ and $\text{fee}_0(n)$ are in order before proceeding to the formal model. Recall that in Chapter 4, the probability of retention in the second period was formulated as a function of C and α. In addition, it was suggested (in Chapter 4, footnote 11) that, when audit quality is allowed to vary, the probability of retention in the second period is also a function of θ, i.e.,

$$\phi_R = \phi_R(\alpha, C, \theta).$$

In the current model, we have written ϕ_R as a function of n, the number of two period audit clients of the auditor. These two formulations are consistent with each other because the solution of the auditor's choice problem determines an optimal value of n, n^*, which is a function of the contractual attributes, α, C, and θ.[8] Thus, the probability of retention of the auditor in the second period can be expressed as

$$\phi_R = \phi_R(n^*(\alpha, C, \theta))$$

where an asterisk denotes the optimal (chosen) value of n.

Similarly, $\text{fee}_0(n^*)$ is also a function of the contractual attributes, α, C, and θ because of its functional dependence on n^*. Later in this section, we show that, as the number of two period audit clients increases, auditors become less likely to attest falsely to the financial statements of a given client. The initial audit fee is a function of the auditor's perceived independence; in effect auditors with relatively greater n^* are supplying their clients with a higher level of audit quality (i.e., a lower assessed probability of false attestation). Therefore, because audit quality increases in n, it must be the case that

$$\partial \text{ fee}_0(n^*)/\partial n > 0.$$

Any given auditor in this model is characterized by his chosen n^*, which serves to summarize the auditor's perceived independence from clients.

Given the definitions and assumptions of the model, the auditor's profit maximization problem can be formulated as

$$\underset{n}{\text{maximize }} \pi^i(n) = n_0[\text{fee}_0(n) - wA_0 - \frac{\phi_R(n)\theta(C+\alpha wA_0)}{(1+r)}] - c^i(n) \quad (1)$$

which asserts that auditors will choose n in order to maximize the present value of expected profits over both time periods. The first order condition for maximization is that

$$\pi^i_n = \text{fee}_0 - wA_0 + [\phi_R + n\frac{\partial \phi_R}{\partial n}]\frac{\theta(C+\alpha wA_0)}{(1+r)} - c^i_n$$

$$+ n\frac{\partial \text{ fee}_0}{\partial n} = 0 \quad (2)$$

Equation (2) is the optimality condition that the auditor will increase n, the number of $T=2$ clients, until the marginal costs of increasing n equal the marginal benefits. In addition, we assume that the sufficient second order condition for profit maximization is satisfied, i.e., that

$$\pi^i_{nn} = [2\frac{\partial \phi_R}{\partial n} + n \frac{\partial^2 \phi_R}{\partial n^2}]\frac{\theta(C+\alpha wA_0)}{(1+r)}$$
$$- c^i_{nn} + [2\frac{\partial \text{fee}_0}{\partial n} + n \frac{\partial^2 \text{fee}_0}{\partial n^2}] < 0 \qquad (3)$$

which says that total revenues must be increasing at a slower rate than are total costs.

The solution of the first order condition, equation (2), results in an optimal (chosen) value:

$$n = n^*(\alpha, C, \theta)$$

where n^* is expressed as a function of the contractual attributes. Substitution of this optimal value of n into the objective function yields the indirect objective function:

$$\pi^i(n^*) = n^*[\text{fee}_0(n^*) - wA_0 - \frac{\phi_R(n^*)\theta(C+\alpha wA_0)}{(1+r)}] - c^i(n^*) \qquad (4)$$

In general, auditors with differing coordination costs will choose different values for n^*. However, as long as perfect substitutes exist for every auditor in the initial period, competition ensures that all auditors will expect to earn zero profits at equilibrium, over both time periods combined (but not in each time period). This zero profit condition is that equation (4) be zero for all i. Initial audit fees will adjust to maintain this condition, as they did in the Chapter 4 model.

Setting (4) equal to zero and solving for $\text{fee}_0(n^*)$ yields

$$\text{fee}_0(n^*) = wA_0 - \frac{\phi_R(n^*)\theta(C+\alpha wA_0)}{(1+r)} + \frac{c^i(n^*)}{n^*} \qquad (5)$$

Initial audit fees will differ across auditors as the costs of coordination, and therefore n^*, differ across auditors. Fees differ because the audit quality supplied by auditors differs. The fee which an auditor characterized by $n=n^*$ can charge is determined by the interaction of supply and demand in the marketplace to be $\text{fee}_0(n^*)$. Absent costs of discovering prices, an auditor who sets a higher fee will gain zero clients; one who sets a lower fee will attract all clients in the market. The equilibrium audit fee at time zero will thus be $\text{fee}_0(n^*)$

and n^* will be chosen such that the expected present value of audit fees, $\pi^i(n^*)$, is zero for all auditors.

The comparative statics predictions of the model are obtained by differentiating the first order condition (2) with respect to the parameters of interest, the contractual attributes α, C, and θ. First, expressing the first order condition (2) as a function of the choice variable n^* and the parameter C, we get the identity

$$\frac{\partial \pi^i(n^*, C)}{\partial n} \equiv 0 \qquad (2a)$$

Taking the total derivative of (2a) with respect to C yields

$$\frac{d}{dC}\left[\frac{\partial \pi^i(n^*, C)}{\partial n}\right] = \frac{\partial^2 \pi^i}{\partial n^2} \cdot \frac{\partial n^*}{\partial C} + \frac{\partial^2 \pi^i}{\partial n \partial C} \equiv 0$$

and

$$\frac{\partial n^*}{\partial \alpha} = -\frac{\partial^2 \pi^i / \partial n^2}{\partial^2 \pi^i / \partial n^2}$$

$$= \frac{-\dfrac{\theta}{(1+r)}\left[\phi_R + n^* \dfrac{\partial \phi_R}{\partial n}\right]}{\left[2\dfrac{\partial \phi_R}{\partial n} + n^* \dfrac{\partial^2 \phi_R}{\partial n^2}\right]\dfrac{\theta(C + \alpha w A_0)}{(1+r)} + \left[2\dfrac{\partial \text{fee}_0}{\partial n} + n^* \dfrac{\partial^2 \text{fee}_0}{\partial n^2}\right] - c_{nn}^i}$$

$$> 0 \qquad (6)$$

Assuming that the sufficient second order condition is satisfied, the denominator of equation (6) is negative. In the numerator of (6), the term $[\phi_R + n^*(\partial \phi_R/\partial n)]$ is $d/dn\,[n^*\phi_R(n^*)]$, the change in the expected number of two period clients as the chosen number of two period clients changes. With rational expectations, auditors will only increase n^* if $n^*\phi_R(n^*)$ increases as well, and thus the term $[\phi_R + n^*(\partial \phi_R/\partial n)] > 0$. Therefore, both the numerator and the denominator of equation (6) are negative and $\partial n^*/\partial C > 0$ can be signed unambiguously. Equation (6) says that, ceteris paribus, as the transaction costs of changing auditors increase, auditors will attempt to increase the number of $T=2$ time horizon clients.

Now, while all auditors will have the incentive to increase n^* when C increases, all auditors cannot be successful at increasing the number of $T=2$ audit clients, if the total number of clients in the market is fixed. Increased competition among auditors for a fixed number of clients implies that the marginal auditors (those for whom $c^i(n)$ are relatively high) will earn negative profits after the increase in C (and after adjustments in $n*$). These marginal auditors cannot sustain negative profits in the long run, and thus will eventually be forced to exit the market for audit services. The result will be increased auditor concentration, i.e., fewer auditors (than before the change) with, on average, a greater number of audit clients. Therefore, one potentially testable implication of this model is

> H_3: *Ceteris paribus,* auditors have, on average, increased the number of their audit clients in the time period subsequent to Securities Release #34-9344 and ASR-165. Furthermore, the number of auditors has decreased in the same time period.[9]

Similarly, differentiating the first order condition with respect to α yields the prediction that

$$\frac{\partial n^*}{\partial \alpha} = \frac{-\partial^2 \pi^i / \partial n \partial \alpha}{\partial^2 \pi^i / \partial n^2}$$

$$= \frac{-\frac{\theta w A_0}{(1+r)}[\phi_R + n^* \frac{\partial \phi_R}{\partial n}]}{[2\frac{\partial \phi_R}{\partial n} + n^* \frac{\partial^2 \phi_R}{\partial n^2}]\frac{\theta(C+\alpha w A_0)}{(1+r)} + [2\frac{\partial \text{fee}_0}{\partial n} + n^* \frac{\partial^2 \text{fee}_0}{\partial n^2}] - c^i_{nn}} > 0 \quad (7)$$

Again, assuming that the sufficient second order condition is satisfied, the denominator of equation (7) is negative. By arguments identical to those presented earlier, the numerator is also negative. Therefore, equation (7) is positive, and a testable implication of the model is

> H_4: *Ceteris paribus,* after a change in accounting or auditing standards which has the effect of increasing potential learning-by-doing advantages, auditors have, on average, increased the number of their audit clients. Furthermore, the number of auditors has simultaneously decreased.

Again, as all auditors attempt to increase the number of their audit clients, marginal auditors will be forced to leave the market because audit fees will not increase sufficiently to compensate them for increased costs of coordination associated with increasing $n*$.

Finally, differentiating the first order condition with respect to θ yields the prediction that

$$\frac{\partial n^*}{\partial \theta} = - \frac{\partial^2 \pi^i / \partial n \partial \theta}{\partial^2 \pi^i / \partial n^2}$$

$$= \frac{-\dfrac{(C + \alpha w A_0)}{(1+r)} [\phi_R + n^* \dfrac{\partial \phi_R}{\partial n}]}{[2 \dfrac{\partial \phi_R}{\partial n} + n^* \dfrac{\partial^2 \phi_R}{\partial n^2}] \dfrac{\theta(C + \alpha w A_0)}{(1+r)} + [2 \dfrac{\partial \text{fee}_0}{\partial n} + n^* \dfrac{\partial^2 \text{fee}_0}{\partial n^2}] - c_{nn}^i}$$

$$> 0 \qquad (8)$$

Equation (8) states that, as θ in the model increases for a given auditor, that auditor will attempt to increase the number of $T = 2$ audit clients. A testable implication of (8) is therefore

> H_5: *Ceteris paribus,* subsequent to regulation which had the effect of increasing θ in the model (such as regulation which mandated that firms provide audited financial statements to the public), auditors have, on average, increased the number of their audit clients. Furthermore, the number of auditors has simultaneously decreased.

In other words, as the "bargaining power" of auditors with respect to clients increases, all auditors will attempt to increase the number of two period audit clients. However, all auditors are not equally equipped to increase n^* because of differing costs of coordination. Marginal auditors will earn negative profits subsequent to the change, after all adjustments, and therefore will exit the market. Increased auditor concentration will be the result of a change which has the effect of increasing θ (or α, or C) in the model.

Now suppose that, in the course of the time zero audit, the auditor discovers that client n is in financial trouble. Assume that, if the auditor does not reveal the "truth" at time zero, client n will survive long enough to pay the auditor's time one audit fees. The availability of this strategy presumes that auditors and clients are able to conceal the client's "true" state from investors, at least in the short run. As discussed in Chapter 4, auditors who possess future economic interest in a client have some incentive to attest falsely. The extent to which auditor opportunism of this sort will actually occur, however, is governed by the auditor's perceived marginal costs and benefits of false attestation. The incentive for false attestation is provided by future economic interest in a given client.

There are, however, countervailing incentives provided in this model by the existence of future economic profits from the auditor's other two period clients. If the auditor is discovered to have attested falsely for one client, he stands to lose the present value of the future economic profit from his other clients. For simplicity, we assume that all other $T=2$ clients of this auditor will immediately terminate him if he is caught "cheating."

Given that the client is in financial difficulty and will fail unless the auditor attests falsely, the expected benefit to the auditor of telling the truth can be expressed as

$$EB_T(n^*) = \frac{(n^*-1)\theta(C+\alpha wA_0)}{(1+r)} \qquad (9)$$

which assumes, for simplicity, that all of the other $T=2$ clients of this auditor are solvent and will retain the auditor if he is not caught "cheating."

If the auditor attests falsely to the financial statements of client n and is discovered, by assumption all of his clients will terminate him. Therefore, the expected benefits from attesting falsely can be expressed as

$$EB_L(n^*) = \frac{n^*\theta(C+\alpha wA_0)}{(1+r)}(1 - \phi_C(n^*)) \qquad (10)$$

where $\phi_C(n^*)$ is the exogenous probability of being caught "cheating" on audit quality.[10] We model $\phi_C(n^*)$ as dependent on n^* because it seems reasonable to suppose that the probability of being caught "cheating" increases in the number of long term audit clients. Large audit firms are thus assumed to be subject to a higher level of exogenous monitoring than are small audit firms, i.e.,

$$\frac{\partial \phi_C(n^*)}{\partial n} > 0.$$

Taking the difference between equations (10) and (9) yields the expected net benefit from misrepresenting client n's financial status:[11]

$$ENB_L(n^*) = \frac{\theta(C+\alpha wA_0)}{(1+r)}[1 - n^*\phi_C(n^*)] \qquad (11)$$

Equation (11) illustrates the collateral bond function of n, the total number of $T=2$ clients, where clients are identical and auditors earn future economic profits.[12] Equation (11) has an interesting interpretation. We argued in Chapter 4 that the existence of future economic profit from, say, client n provides the incentive for the auditor to attest falsely to that client's financial statements in certain states of the world. Therefore, the existence of future economic profit from client n impairs auditor independence with respect to client n. On the other hand, the existence of future economic profit from other clients serves to restrain auditor opportunism with respect to client n. In this model, the future economic profit from other clients is what the auditor stands to lose by attesting falsely to the financial statements of client n.

Examining equation (11), we can see that the auditor will "cheat" or not depending on whether (11) is positive or negative. Equation (11) is negative (no "cheating") if the auditor has a sufficiently large number of clients such that

$$n^* > \frac{1}{\phi_C(n^*)}$$

In other words, for n^* sufficiently large, the expected losses from auditor opportunism exceed the expected gains.[13] It can be easily seen that, were $c^i(n) = 0$, there would be benefits but no costs to auditor size. Therefore, $c^i(n) = 0$ would imply that one auditor would exist at equilibrium.

Before analyzing how the expected net benefits of "cheating" change as n^* changes, we examine the Cohen Commission's assertion that there is an important relationship between audit firm size and auditor independence. Specifically, the Cohen Commission argues that

> When one or a few large clients supply a significant portion of the total fees of a public accounting firm, the firm will have greater difficulty in maintaining its independence. The staff study of the Subcommittee on Reports, Accounts and Management (the Metcalf Report), for example, cites the case of a relatively small firm with a single client that represented 30 percent of the firm's total fees in the year 1973. In the celebrated Equity Funding case, that company represented more than 40 percent of the fees of the Wolfson, Weiner firm that audited the parent company. (pp. 113-144)

Expressing equation (11) in terms of (possibly unequal) profits, we get

$$ENB_L(n^*) = \frac{\pi_n}{(1+r)} - \phi_C(n^*) \Sigma_{j=1}^{n^*} \frac{\pi_j}{(1+r)}$$

which says that the auditor's expected net gains from false attestation depend on the difference between the expected economic profit (not total fees) from client n and the expected economic profit from all other clients times the probability of getting caught. Our analysis implies that the Cohen Commission's position is oversimplified, because a client could "supply a significant portion of the total fees of a public accounting firm" and, if future economic profit from the client were zero, the client would pose no threat to independence by the "economic interest" concept.

In order to model differences in audit quality, we are ultimately interested in consumers' evaluations of the probability that the auditor will knowingly misrepresent a given client's financial status. We assume that consumers of audit services use the auditor's chosen n^* as an (imperfect) surrogate for perceived independence from clients. In other words, consumers of audit services are aware that auditors characterized by differing n^* will have different incentives for false attestation. Defining $\phi_L(n^*)$ as consumers' assessment of the probability that an auditor will "cheat" on audit quality, given that he has chosen $n = n^*$, rational expectations dictate that

$$\text{sign} \frac{\partial \phi_L(n^*)}{\partial n} = \text{sign} \frac{\partial ENB_L(n^*)}{\partial n}$$

Differentiating (11) with respect to n yields

$$\frac{\partial ENB_L(n^*)}{\partial n} = - \frac{\theta(C + \alpha w A_0)}{(1+r)} [\phi_C(n^*) + n^* \frac{\partial \phi_C(n^*)}{\partial n}] < 0 \qquad (12)$$

Equation (12) states that the expected net benefits from false attestation decrease as n^* increases. By the logic above,

$$\frac{\partial \phi_L(n^*)}{\partial n} < 0$$

which says that consumers' assessments of the auditor's incentives for false attestation decline as the total number of two period clients of that auditor increases. Therefore, auditors with relatively higher n^* supply their clients with a higher level of audit quality.

To summarize this section: we first modeled the auditor's choice of n, the total number of $T=2$ time horizon clients. The comparative statics predictions of this model are that, ceteris paribus, n^* will increase when

(1) the transactions costs of changing auditors increases for all clients,

(2) firm specific learning-by-doing advantages increase for all clients, or

(3) the auditor's bargaining power with respect to clients increases.

We then analyzed the auditor's decision of whether to attest falsely to the financial statements of a given client. Our model suggests that this decision depends on the probability of getting caught and (with clients which offer identical economic profit at time one), the total number of $T=2$ horizon clients of the auditor. The expected net benefits from "cheating" and thus, with rational expectations, consumers' assessments of the probability of auditor "cheating" decrease as n^* increases. In the following section, we formulate the client's choice of contract length.

5.3 Choice of Length of the Auditor-Client Relationship

In this section, we examine the client's choice of a one period ($T=1$) or a two period ($T=2$) time horizon, i.e., whether to hire a new auditor in the second period or retain the incumbent auditor for the time one audit. We assume that the client has already made the decision to invest in audit services, i.e., that auditing is not a negative net present value investment. Thus, the client's choice problem can be expressed as: given that an audit is to be performed, what is the optimal contractual form to employ? We assert that clients make this choice in order to maximize net firm value from contracting for audit services. Clients and auditors are assumed to contract costlessly for one period ($T=1$) horizons, that is, one period contracts are costlessly enforced. Two period contracts, on the other hand, involve independence costs that are not present with one period contracts. These costs are a result of the bilateral monopoly between auditor and client that obtains at the recontracting interval (time $t=1$). Thus, two period contracts pose contractual problems which are absent from one period contracts.

The timing convention of the model is as follows: at $t=0$, auditors and clients simultaneously solve their decision problems. The solution consists of the choice of $n=n^*$ for all auditors and a set of one period ($T=1$) and two period ($T=2$) contracts between auditors and clients. While one period contracts are costlessly enforced, two period contracts are not, and thus the renewal of $T=2$ contracts is not certain. For example, the $T=2$ clients of a given auditor will, by assumption, terminate the auditor if he is discovered to have "cheated" on audit quality. Thus, renewal of $T=2$ contracts at time one is probabilistic. However, the capital market's expectations about renewal are reflected in the time zero share price of the client who chooses a $T=2$ time horizon.[14]

Define $V_0(T=1)$ as the change in the time zero value of the firm which chooses to contract for audit services in a $T=1$ time horizon (gross of the costs of this strategy). $V_0(T=1)$ depends on the time horizon chosen because, as discussed in Chapter 4, an auditor with no future economic interest in the client has no direct incentive to attest falsely in order to retain this particular client in future periods. $V_0(T=1)$ does not depend on the contractual attributes α, θ, or C because choosing $T=1$ guarantees that audit fees will equal total costs in both time periods. Assume that an exogenously-imposed law makes it prohibitively costly for clients to announce to the market at $t=0$ that $T=1$ is chosen, pay the audit fee at $t=0$ of wA_0 and then contract again with that auditor at time one. In other words, it is prohibitively costly for clients to promise $T=1$ at time zero in order to capture the valuation impact, and then renege on the promise at time one. Then since the auditor chosen at time zero is certain he will not audit the client at time one, he will be unwilling to bid below wA_0 for any audit client. At time one, no new auditor will bid below total cost because time $t=1$ is the last period in the model.[15] Thus, zero profits will be earned by auditors in each time period when the client chooses a $T=1$ time horizon.

We can characterize the net benefits from contracting for audit services with a one period time horizon as incorporated in the client's share price at time zero and equal to

$$\overline{V}(T=1) = V_0(T=1) - wA_0 - [\frac{wA_0+C}{(1+r)}]. \tag{13}$$

Several aspects of $T=1$ time horizons are worthy of note. First, this strategy is the two period analogue to hiring two non-colluding auditors to compete in all future periods. Second, this strategy completely removes the bilateral monopoly and independence problems, albeit at a cost (in higher audit fees). Choosing $T=1$ is the only strategy available in this model which removes the independence problem. Clients can lessen the independence problem in a $T=2$ horizon by choosing an auditor with relatively high n^*, but they cannot remove it entirely because two period contracts are not costlessly negotiated and enforced.

The other strategy available to the client at time zero is to choose a $T=2$ time horizon, i.e., to choose one auditor for both time periods. Clients who choose a two period horizon are assumed to contract explicitly for one period only, but both parties (and the capital market) expect renewal at the recontracting interval with probability $\phi_R(n^*)$. In Chapter 4, we showed that the existence of $\alpha > 0$, $C > 0$, $\theta > 0$ implies that the auditor has a future economic interest in the client. This is true because the auditor is able to use the comparative cost advantage from performing the client's time zero audit to capture profits greater than zero at time one. This economic interest provides the auditor with the incentive to "cheat" at time zero in certain states of the world. The auditor who has an economic interest in supplying the client's $t=1$ audit services is more likely to misrepresent the client's financial status at $t=0$. Rational agents at $t=0$ will forecast this incentive on the part of incumbent auditors and, in an efficient capital market, the client's share price will fully reflect the potential for misrepresentation. While a large number of other $T=2$ audit clients reduces the auditor's incentive to "cheat," it does not remove it. Thus, if $V_0(T=2)$ is defined as the (gross of costs) change in client firm value at time zero if a two period horizon is chosen, rational expectations will dictate that

$$V_0(T=2) < V_0(T=1).$$

$V_0(T=2)$ is a function not only of the chosen contract length, but also of the auditor's perceived independence from clients. As argued above, consumers of audit services evaluate the probability of false attestation, $\phi_L(n)$, on the part of the incumbent auditor by observation of n^*. The auditor's chosen number of two period clients is, in turn, a function of the contractual attributes α, C, and θ. To express this functional dependence, we can write

$$V_0(T=2) = V_0(T=2, \phi_L(n^*(\alpha, C, \theta)))$$

where $\partial V_0(T=2, \phi_L)/\partial \phi_L < 0$. The market's valuation of the benefits of an audit will decrease as the probability that the auditor will attest falsely increases.

In an efficient capital market, $V_0(T=2, \phi_L)$ will fully reflect the ex ante benefits of contracting for audit services in a two period horizon. The total costs of this strategy are the audit fees at time zero plus the present value of expected audit fees at time one. Recall from Section 5.2 that the time zero audit fee is

$$\text{fee}_0(n^*) = wA_0 - \frac{\phi_R(n^*)\,\theta\,(C+\alpha wA_0)}{(1+r)} + \frac{c^i(n^*)}{n^*}$$

The client's expected audit fee at time one will be the probability of retaining the incumbent auditor times his fee plus one minus the probability of retention times a new auditor's fee plus the costs of changing auditors:

$$E^j\frac{(\text{fee}_1)}{(1+r)} = \phi_R[\frac{\theta\,(C+\alpha wA_0) + wA_1}{(1+r)}] + (1-\phi_R(n^*))\,[\frac{wA_0 + C}{(1+r)}]$$

Therefore, the expected net benefits from contracting for audit services over a two period time horizon can be expressed as

$$\overline{V}(T=2, \phi_L(n^*)) = V_0(T=2, \phi_L(n^*)) - wA_0 - \frac{c^i(n^*)}{n^*} \qquad (14)$$

$$+ \frac{\phi_R(n^*)\,(C+\alpha wA_0)}{(1+r)} - [\frac{wA_0 + C}{(1+r)}]$$

70   The Auditor-Client Relationship

In order to compare the expected net benefits under each strategy, define $D(n^*)$ as the difference between equations (14) and (13):

$$D(n^*) = \overline{V}(T=2, \phi_L(n^*)) - \overline{V}(T=1)$$
$$= [V_0(T=2, \phi_L(n^*)) - V_0(T=1)] + [\frac{\phi_R(n^*)(C+\alpha wA_0)}{(1+r)} - \frac{c^i(n^*)}{n^*}] \quad (15)$$

Equation (15) says that the difference in the client's expected net benefits from choosing $T=2$ and $T=1$ time horizons is composed of two elements. The first term in brackets is the negative impact on client firm value of choosing a two period over a one period contractual relationship. The second term in brackets equals the present value of the cost savings of retaining the incumbent auditor at time one.

Equation (15) captures the relevant tradeoffs involved in the client's choice of time horizon. Intuitively, choosing one auditor for both time periods economizes on audit fees. On the other hand, since an incumbent auditor ($\alpha, \theta, C > 0$) has the incentive to "cheat" at $t=0$ in certain states of the world in order to keep the client, there is a negative impact on client firm value of maintaining a continuous relationship with one auditor. This impact on client value is the explicit cost of impaired auditor independence.

Clients can mitigate this effect somewhat by contracting with auditors who possess a large number of other $T=2$ time horizon clients. This strategy, however, is not costless because of positive costs of coordinating a large number of two period audit clients. To see this, examine equation (15) in order to ascertain the effect of an increase in n^*. Intuitively, an increase in n^* would increase the client firm's market value from a two period contract because it decreases the probability that the auditor will misrepresent the client's financial condition. On the other hand, an increase in n^* will also affect the second term in (15), the present value of the cost savings from retaining the incumbent auditor. It is this latter effect which represents the cost of choosing an auditor with a relatively large n^* in the model. Clients will trade off the marginal benefits and costs of increasing n^* and, at equilibrium, will equate the two.

Because $V_0(T=1)$ does not depend on n, the client's choice problem can be separated into two subdecisions. First, in order to maximize firm value from contracting for audit services, the client will choose an auditor who is characterized by a chosen number of audit clients. Second, after choosing the optimal $T=2$ auditor, the client will choose either $T=2$ or $T=1$, depending on which choice maximizes net firm value from contracting for audit services. Since firm value maximization is equivalent to choosing n^* in order to maximize $D(n^*)$, the first decicion can be expressed as

$$\text{maximize } D(n^*) = [V_0(T=2, \phi_L(n^*)) - V_0(T=1)]$$
$$+ \left[\frac{\phi_R(n^*)(C + \alpha w A_0)}{(1+r)} - \frac{c^i(n^*)}{n^*}\right] \quad (16)$$

The simultaneous solution of the client's and the auditor's decision problem results in the optimal value of n^*, denote it $\hat{n}^*$. Substituting this value into equation (16) yields the indirect objective function:

$$D(\hat{n}^*) = [V_0(T=2, \phi_L(\hat{n}^*)) - V_0(T=1)]$$
$$+ \left[\frac{\phi_R(\hat{n}^*)(C + \alpha w A_0)}{(1+r)} - \frac{c^i(\hat{n}^*)}{\hat{n}^*}\right] \quad (17)$$

Once the optimal value of $\hat{n}^*$ is determined, the second step is for the client to choose either a one period or a two period contractual relationship. We can characterize the optimum by the client's decision rule:

$$\text{Choose } T = 2 \text{ horizon if } D(\hat{n}^*) > 0$$
$$\text{Choose } T = 1 \text{ horizon if } D(\hat{n}^*) < 0$$

Examining equation (17), we can see that, by assumption, the first term in brackets is negative, and is equal to the loss in client firm value implied by retaining the incumbent auditor for the time one audit. The second term in brackets is positive and equals the present value of the expected cost savings at time one due to retaining the incumbent auditor at that time.

The comparative statics predictions of the model emerge when we differentiate (17) with respect to C and α. First, differentiating (17) with respect to C yields

$$\frac{dD(\hat{n}^*)}{dC} = \frac{\partial D(\hat{n}^*)}{\partial C} = \frac{\phi_R(\hat{n}^*)}{(1+r)} > 0 \quad (18)$$

by the Envelope Theorem.[16] Equation (18) predicts that, as the transactions costs of changing auditors increase, clients will be more likely to choose longer relationships with their auditors. Intuitively, at the optimum, clients have chosen $n = \hat{n}^*$ such that the marginal benefits of choosing an auditor characterized by $\hat{n}^*$ audit clients exactly offset the marginal costs of that strategy. For small changes around the optimum, then, varying the choice variable has zero marginal effect on the objective function. Thus the total change is captured by the effect of varying the parameter alone, in this case, the transactions costs of changing auditors.

Similarly, differentiating (17) with respect to α yields

$$\frac{dD(\hat{n}*)}{d\alpha} = \frac{\partial D(\hat{n}*)}{\partial \alpha} = \frac{\phi_R(\hat{n}*)\, wA_0}{(1+r)} > 0 \qquad (19)$$

by the Envelope Theorem. Equation (19) predicts that, as learning-by-doing advantages increase for all clients, clients will be more likely to choose longer relationships with their auditors. Intuitively, the net effect of an increase in learning-by-doing advantages is an increase in the cost savings of retaining the incumbent auditor. As the cost savings increase, ceteris paribus, clients will be more likely to retain one auditor for both time periods.

In summary, in this section we have developed a model of the client's choice of auditor and the length of the auditor-client relationship. This model generates two testable implications: when the auditor has a sufficiently large number of audit clients, the average length of the auditor-client relationship will increase when, ceteris paribus,

(1) the transactions costs of changing auditors increase for all clients, or

(2) learning-by-doing advantages increase for all clients.

In the following section, we formulate these hypotheses in testable form and review extant evidence bearing on these predictions.

5.4 Testable Implications and Extant Evidence

The comparative statics implications of this chapter's model generate several testable hypotheses. The first three hypotheses emerge from the auditor's choice problem and are time-series predictions about auditor concentration in the market for audit services. Specifically, the model predicts that, as either the costs of changing auditors, learning-by-doing advantages, or auditors' bargaining position with respect to clients increases, auditor concentration will also increase in the market. By an increase in concentration, we mean that, at equilibrium, a fewer number of auditors will exist with a greater average number of audit clients.

No comprehensive study of changes in auditor concentration over time has been published to date. Extant studies are confined to auditor concentration within certain industries, and with respect to large client firms only. Furthermore, these studies have concentrated exclusively on the "Big 8"/non-"Big 8" dichotomy. Several of the studies on auditor industry concentration are reviewed in Chapter 6.

The client's choice problem yields two additional hypotheses which predict differences in the length of the auditor-client relationship. The first hypothesis follows from equation (18):

$$\frac{dD(\hat{n}^*)}{dC} = \frac{\partial D(\hat{n}^*)}{\partial C} = \frac{\phi_R(\hat{n}^*)}{(1+r)} > 0$$

and can be expressed as the time-series prediction that:

H_6: *Ceteris paribus*, the rate at which client firms change auditors has, on average, decreased in the period subsequent to

(1) Securities Release No. 34-9344, effective on October 31, 1971, and

(2) ASR-165, effective on January 1, 1975.

We use observed auditor change rates here as a proxy for expected auditor change rates, given the choice of the optimal contract length.[17]

There is some extant empirical evidence bearing on H_6. Coe and Palmon [1979] looked at auditor changes (of all types) for two samples: the first was a sample of 726 companies from the COMPUSTAT index over the twenty-four year period from 1952-1975. These firms comprise what Coe and Palmon call the audit services market for larger firms. The second was a sample of approximately 10,000 firms subject to SEC requirements from the *Disclosure Journal* for the two years 1974 and 1975. This second sample includes small and medium-sized, as well as large firms. Coe and Palmon examine two change rates:

Type A: All auditor changes including mergers of CPA firms.

Type B: All auditor changes excluding mergers of CPA firms.

For the first (large firm) sample, they report the following results:

Year	Type A Rate	Type B Rate
1974	2.47%	2.20%
1975	2.34%.	2.34%

The Type B data do not appear to be consistent with H_6. However, later in the paper, Coe and Palmon report the following results for OTC firms from the first sample and all firms from the second:

Year	OTC Type A	SEC Sample
1974	3.48%	5.4%
1975	1.14%	2.7%

Coe and Palmon interpret these results as follows:

> In both cases, the turnover rate of 1974 exceeded that of 1975. The larger 1974 turnover rates may be related to the economic recession of 1974 where there was a larger than average bankruptcy rate. (p. 11)

Contrary to Coe and Palmon's explanation, our analysis seeks to attribute the time-series difference in auditor change rates to regulation effective January 1, 1975 (ASR-165) which made it more costly for firms to change auditors.

Wallace [1979], in her discussant's comments on Coe and Palmon, reports the following number of auditor changes per the *Disclosure Journal:*

Time Period	Total Number of Auditor Changes
1/73-4/73	168 (data for three months only)
5/73-4/74	547
5/74-4/75	619
5/75-4/76	226

In order to get a better idea of the behavior of auditor change rates before and after ASR-165, we inspected the *Disclosure Journals* of 1973-1974 and 1974-1975. Incorporating the three sources of information (Coe-Palmon, Wallace, and the *Disclosure Journals*), we discovered that the number of auditor changes for firms reporting to the SEC were

1973:	573
1974:	542
1975:	277

These data appear to be consistent with the hypothesis that firms change auditors less frequently subsequent to the effective date of ASR-165 than they did prior to that date.

In general, auditor change rates appear to be decreasing over the time period 1973-1976. This observation is consistent with the results of two Financial Executives' Institute studies. These studies found that, for the 1971 survey data, 10% of the U.S. firms changed auditors over the prior three years (annualized rate: 3.3%). For the 1977 survey data, 14% of the U.S. respondents changed auditors over the previous five years (annualized rate: 2.8%). However, in addition to the problems caused by aggregation of these data over three and five year periods, it is not clear how firms which changed auditors more than once in any period are treated. Furthermore, in order to constitute a test of H_6, the data would have to be partitioned around the event of interest. The FEI results are, however, consistent with a general decline in auditor change rates over the time period 1968-1976.

Another interesting statistic is the time-series behavior of the number of auditor-client disagreements actually reported to the SEC from 1971 to the present. *The CPA Letter* of October 15, 1979 reports the number of disagreements filed with the SEC on Form 8-K for the years 1974 through 1978. The letter asserts that the data show a declining trend in the number of reported auditor-client disagreements. Reproduced below are the total number of disagreements and the total number of companies reporting disagreements for the years 1974-1978.

Year	Number of Disagreements	Number of Firms
1974	52	33
1975	87	50
1976	69	55
1977	47	32
1978	42	32

For the years 1974 and 1975, we can combine the data from *The CPA Letter* and the *Disclosure Journal* in order to express the number of disagreements reported to the SEC as a percentage of total number of reported auditor changes. For the years 1974 and 1975, this percentage is

        1974:   9.6% reported
        1975:   31.4% reported

Using a chi-square test for differences, the value of the corrected chi-square statistic, $X_c^2 = 52.85$, is significant at the .005 level. We can conclude that the ratio of reported disagreements to auditor changes increased significantly between the years 1974 and 1975. Although causality is not an implication of the test, the data are consistent with the hypothesis that one effect of ASR-165 was to increase the percentage of auditor changes which required SEC disclosure, thereby increasing the costs to firms of changing auditors.

To summarize the discussion of H_6: extant empirical evidence is weakly consistent with the general observation that auditor change rates have declined in the time period 1968-1978. In order to provide a rigorous test of H_6, the data would have to be more carefully partitioned around the events of interest, Securities Release No. 34-9344 and ASR-165. Currently available evidence is also consistent with the hypothesis that ASR-165 has been effective in increasing the ratio of reported disagreements to auditor changes for the years 1974 and 1975.

A second potentially testable implication of the model follows directly from equation (19):

$$\frac{dD(\hat{n}^*)}{d\alpha} = \frac{\partial D(\hat{n}^*)}{\partial \alpha} = \frac{\phi_R(\hat{n}^*)wA_0}{(1+r)} > 0$$

For an increase in the start-up costs of auditing on all clients, we would expect to observe lower auditor change rates, ceteris paribus. An example of a simultaneous change in α for all firms would be the implementation of a new auditing or reporting standard, such as a requirement that auditors report on the state of a firm's internal control system, or the provision of audited segment or general price level information. This hypothesis can be stated formally as

H_7: *Ceteris paribus,* the rate at which client firms change auditors is, on average, lower subsequent to the implementation of an accounting or auditing standard which had the effect of raising the start-up costs of auditing.

A test of H_7 could be accomplished by choosing an accounting or auditing standard which appeared to have raised auditing start-up costs, and examining auditor change rates for affected firms before and after its implementation. Since casual empiricism suggests that such standards are increasing over time, H_7 would be consistent with extant evidence that auditor change rates are declining over time.

To summarize this chapter: we initially discussed the use of explicit and implicit contracting for the exchange of audit services. We then formulated the auditor's choice problem with respect to the number of long term clients and analyzed the auditor's incentives to "cheat" on audit quality. We showed that auditor opportunism is constrained by the existence of future economic profit from other audit clients. In the client's choice problem of contract length, we allowed audit quality to vary by modeling the quality dimension of audit services as the impact of the contractual attributes on client firm value. These models yield several testable implications which were enumerated in the last section of the chapter. In that section, we also examined extant empirical evidence bearing on some of these predictions. In the following chapter, we extend the model to incorporate the auditor's knowledge of client industry, i.e., potential learning-by-doing advantages at the industry level.

6

Economies in Audit Technology and Auditor Industry Specialization

The formal models developed in Chapters 4 and 5 have assumed that auditor knowledge can be partitioned into two mutually exclusive and exhaustive subsets:

(1) General knowledge applicable in auditing all potential clients, and

(2) Specialized knowledge applicable to auditing one particular client.

In actuality, there are likely to be economies in audit technology within certain groups of clients. These economies may arise because of operational and organizational similarities within an industry, industry-specific accounting or auditing standards, or regulation which affects a group of client firms in a similar manner. For simplicity, we refer to groups of clients for which audit economies potentially exist as an industry, while recognizing that this definition of industry differs from common usage. In addition, then, to general and client-specific knowledge of auditing, a third type of knowledge is likely to be important in the exchange of audit services: knowledge of the industry in which a given client operates. The effect of industry-specific knowledge, i.e., learning-by-doing at the industry level, on the portfolio of clients held by auditors is the subject of the current chapter.

When firm-specific learning-by-doing advantages exist, auditor independence may be impaired by the accepted concept (see Chapter 4). However, because there are potential benefits to be gained from auditor independence, both contractual parties have the incentive to contract in a manner which minimizes the impact of specialized assets. One possibility is for auditors to increase the number of audit clients in order to increase the "collateral bond" effect of these clients and thereby decrease the probability of false attestation on any given client (see Chapter 5). When learning-by-doing advantages are also present at the industry level, another potential strategy is to change the number of audit clients within a given industry.

From the auditor's point of view, the existence of industry level learning-by-doing advantages provides an alternative use for what would otherwise be client-specific knowledge. For example, if a fast food chain like McDonald's were to terminate their auditor, it is likely that the auditor could profitably employ some of the experience gained from auditing McDonald's in future audits of another fast food chain, say, Wendy's. If a given client terminates the auditor, he can no longer impose on him a capital loss equal to the entire present value of (higher) future audit fees attributable to this knowledge; the auditor can recoup part of the investment by using the knowledge to reduce the costs of auditing other clients (and potential clients) within the industry.

On the other hand, the existence of potential industry level advantages lowers the alternative supply price for audit services in future time periods. While the existence of industry learning allows a given auditor to lower his costs on other industry clients, it also enables his competitors to lower their costs as well. Whether a given auditor is "better off" after a parameter shift which has the effect of increasing industry-level learning-by-doing advantages depends on whether the change has improved his position relative to his competitors, or has improved their position relative to him.

This effect differs from the effect of an increase in firm-specific learning-by-doing in the following way: an increase in firm-specific knowledge decreases the incumbent auditor's marginal costs of auditing a given client in the second period without changing the marginal benefits (because the marginal costs of the auditor's competitors remain the same, and thus the alternative supply price is unchanged). The analysis of an increase in industry-level learning-by-doing advantages is more complex because the effect is both to lower the incumbent auditor's marginal costs on this and other clients and to lower simultaneously his competitor's marginal costs, thus lowering the incumbent auditor's marginal benefits on this and other clients. Intuitively, whether subsequent to increased industry learning, a given auditor has the incentive to expand the number of clients within that industry depends on whether his increased cost advantages exceed those of his competitors.

The organization of the chapter is as follows: in Section 6.1, we provide an intuitive explanation of the economic forces which drive an auditor to specialize in a given industry. Current regulatory and professional interest in auditor industry specialization is also examined. In Section 6.2, a formal model of auditor specialization is presented, in which we incorporate the choice of client composition where some clients possess industry-level learning-by-doing advantages and others do not. This model generates testable implications about auditor industry specialization as a response to variation in industry learning-by-doing advantages. In Section 6.4, extant evidence on auditor specialization by client industry is reviewed.

6.1 Industry-Level Learning in Auditing

Economies may arise in audit technology for several reasons. First, operational and organizational similarities may exist within a group of client firms. Second, accounting and auditing practices may differ across industries. Third, regulation by industry groups may result in commonalities within the group, but differences across groups.[1] Auditing texts generally assert that knowledge of the industry in which a given client operates is essential background information for auditors. For example, Arens and Loebbecke [1976] state that

> To adequately interpret the meaning of information obtained throughout the audit, an understanding of the *client's industry* is essential. Certain unique aspects of different industries must be reflected in the financial statements. An audit for a life insurance company could not be performed with due care without an understanding of the unique characteristics of the life insurance business. And imagine attempting to audit a client in the bridge construction industry without understanding the construction business and the percentage-of-completion method of accounting. (p. 120)

This quotation highlights two of the reasons for the existence of industry learning advantages. First, client firms may possess common elements in audit technology because of the nature of the industry itself. For example, banks present unique cash control problems. Second, accounting principles or procedures may vary by industry as with, for example, the gas and oil industry.

Casual empiricism would suggest that significant variation exists in accounting and auditing practices across industries. For example, the American Institute of Certified Public Accountants currently publishes four industry accounting guides, 19 industry audit guides, and 29 Statements of Position on specialized practices. In addition, some accounting standards relate only to specific industries (FASB-19 and the petroleum industry), while others specifically exempt certain industries (FASB-12 on accounting for marketable equity securities and mutual life insurance companies). Furthermore, many of the largest public accounting firms have committees and/or partners which are specifically designated as industry specialists.

Another reason for the existence of industry-level learning-by-doing is regulation. Regulated industries are generally required to report their activities to the regulatory body in a mandated format. This format will differ across industries, but will be similar for firms within the industry. Once an auditor has become familiar with the requirements of the regulation, he can profitably employ this knowledge to reduce the costs of auditing other clients within the industry group. The effect on auditors of increased regulation at the industry level is discussed in a recent study by Arnett and Danos [1979]:

> ... many complex regulations are often applicable only to entities in a given industry group, and these regulations often are similar regardless of the size of any individual entity in the group (as is the case with banking) ...
>
> Size, complexity, and regulation demand specialists, making it economically desirable, even essential, for CPA firms to seek significant numbers of clients in a single industry group. To expand on preceding statements, a firm could not, for example, afford to have a specialist well-versed in all the rules and regulations pertaining to utilities if it had only one client in that field; nor could it afford a specialist in estate planning if only one client needed that service. (p. 18)

Again, economies in audit technology are likely to arise because of similarities within a group of client firms caused by operational and organizational similarities, common accounting/auditing procedures, and regulation.

By themselves, audit economies can be expected to lead to industry specialization by auditors. Both the Cohen Commission and the Metcalf Subcommittee devoted resources to this issue. Specifically, the Cohen Report alleges that

> Different industries vary enough in complexity that public accounting firms tend toward industry specialization. If a client is acquired in one industry, there will be pressure to acquire additional clients in the same industry. (p. 112)
>
> The recent congressional staff study (Metcalf Report) indicated that a degree of industry concentration exists in auditing; that is, some public accounting firms audit a substantial proportion of the major companies in particular industries. (p. 113)

The concern of the Metcalf Subcommittee was that auditor concentration within certain industries might be "anti-competitive." According to the Metcalf Report,

> The extensive influence maintained by a "Big Eight"[2] accounting firm over the financial success of a corporate client in one particular industry may also exist for one or more corporate clients in the same industry.
>
> The "Big Eight" firms not only concentrate their influence among major competitors in a single industry, but spread their concentrated influence through other major industries. Independent auditing is one service required by all major corporate competitors in all industries. The spread of "Big Eight" firm concentration through major industries is one of the primary factors contributing to the vast size and influence of the "Big Eight" firms. (p. 44)

Because of potential anti-trust implications of the Metcalf Subcommittee allegations, the existence and potential impact of auditor industry specialization is an important research topic. Extant evidence on auditor industry specialization is reviewed in Section 6.3.

So far in this section, we have provided a rationale for the existence of learning-by-doing at the industry level. By itself, absent significant costs of industry specialization, the existence of industry learning implies auditor monopoly by industry. We do not observe monopolist auditors in various industries (see the literature reviewed in Section 6.3), although we do observe a degree of auditor specialization. Therefore, we can conclude that some other economic forces must exist which provide auditors with a disincentive to specialize by industry.

Arnett and Danos [1979] claim that one such countervailing force is an auditor's desire to diversify his portfolio of clients in order to dampen the business cycle fluctuations of a small number of industries. They claim that the joint effect of industry learning and benefits to client diversification provides large audit firms with a comparative advantage over small audit firms:

> Large firms have the necessary personnel and clients to be able to specialize in a number of different industries. Thus they can reap the benefits of specialization and diversification at the same time. Smaller firms often do not have enough total clients and firm personnel to do this. If they diversify into industries which are highly regulated, they frequently do not have a broad enough base of clients in each such industry to justify the heavy economic and financial commitment required for specialization. (p. 70)

Thus, one countervailing force may be the existence of potential benefits to industry diversification.

Another countervailing force is the existence of "confidentiality" costs. Auditors are privy to sensitive information about clients which, if revealed to that client's competitors, may be very costly to the client. For example, client firms which are engaged in innovation-type activities (such as oil and gas exploration) may be particularly sensitive to this issue. Client firms concerned with confidentiality may not wish to engage an auditor whose other clients are close competitors. We would expect that confidentiality costs are more important in smaller industry groups, and in industries where innovation is relatively more important.

The existence of confidentiality costs and potential benefits to diversification provides auditors with a disincentive to specialize by industry. Offsetting this are potential learning-by-doing advantages at the industry level. A theory which predicts a greater (lesser) degree of auditor specialization becomes testable when we isolate those industries in which the marginal benefits (marginal costs) of specialization are relatively greater. In the following section, a formal model which incorporates the costs and benefits of auditor industry specialization is developed.

6.2 A Formal Model of Auditor Industry Specialization

Like the earlier models in Chapters 4 and 5, the current model is a two period one, with time periods $t=0$ and $t=1$. At time $t=0$, auditors and clients simultaneously solve their respective decision problems, resulting in a set of contractual relationships. At time $t=1$, clients either recontract with the incumbent auditor for one additional audit engagement, or contract with a new auditor for the time $t=1$ audit. Contracts at time $t=1$ are assumed to be perfectly enforceable in order to avoid last period problems (see Chapter 3). Contracting with one auditor for both the time zero and the time one audits entails independence problems induced by the bilateral monopoly situation at the recontracting interval (see Chapter 4). Contracting with a new auditor in each time period avoids these problems, but at the cost of a higher present value of audit fees. In short, the tradeoff which the client faces is the same as that which he faced in the Chapter 5 model except that, in the current model, learning-by-doing advantages at the industry level are assumed to exist for some clients.

In this section, we are concerned with the auditor's choice of

n, the number of two period time horizon clients (for whom no industry economies are assumed to exist), and

l, the number of two period time horizon clients within an industry in which industry level learning-by-doing advantages are present.

Unlike the Chapter 4 and 5 models, the transactions costs of changing auditors are assumed to be zero in order to simplify the analysis. Auditors, as before, are assumed to be identical except for differential costs of coordinating a number of clients. These costs increase as the number of two period ($T=2$) audit clients increases. Coordination costs may differ depending on whether or not the client is a member of the industry group. In order to accommodate these differences, we formulate two cost functions:

$c^i(n)$ = the costs to auditor i of coordinating n two-period audit clients, for whom industry-level learning-by-doing advantages are zero. As in Chapter 5, $c_n^i > 0$, $c_{nn}^i > 0$, where c_n^i is the first derivative of $c^i(n)$ with respect to n, and c_{nn}^i is the second derivative.

$c^i(l)$ = the costs to auditor i of coordinating l two-period audit clients for whom industry-level learning-by-doing advantages are assumed to exist.[3] Coordination costs are such that $c_{ll}^i > 0$.

Clients are assumed to belong to one of two mutually exclusive and exhaustive groups:

Group 1 is a pool of potential audit clients with no industry-level learning-by-doing advantages. Auditor knowledge which can be used to audit these clients is either completely general (usable on all clients) or entirely firm-specific (useful on only one client). As in Chapter 5, the auditor's task is to choose a two-period contractual relationship with n of these clients.

Group 2 is a pool of potential audit clients within an industry whose members share common accounting or auditing characteristics. Auditor knowledge which can be used to audit these clients is of three types:

(1) general knowledge, applicable to both group one and group two clients,

(2) firm-specific knowledge, applicable only on the time $t=1$ audit of the client firm on which it was acquired, and

(3) industry knowledge, applicable to audits of those clients in the second group only.

The auditor's task is to choose a two-period contractual relationship with l of the industry clients.

Clients within group one or two are assumed to be identical. As before, auditors and clients are assumed to be risk neutral, and other quality-guaranteeing arrangements are prohibitively costly.

For both groups of clients, α indexes firm-specific learning-by-doing advantages where

$$0 < \alpha < 1$$

On initial audit engagements, all auditors must input A_0 hours of auditor time on all clients, regardless of industry affiliation.[4] At time zero in the model, all audits are initial engagements, and therefore every auditor supplies A_0 to his client. At time one, if the auditor has previously audited the client, his time input requirement will decrease because of firm-specific learning-by-doing advantages. As before, define

$$A_1 = (1 - \alpha) A_0 = \text{the incumbent auditor's time input at } t=1.$$

In addition, A_1 and αA_0 are substitutable inputs at $t=1$, where $\partial A_1/\partial \alpha = -A_0 < 0$ which says that, as firm-specific learning-by-doing advantages increase, the auditor's time input requirements at $t=1$ decrease on that particular client. Intuitively, the incumbent auditor can use the firm-specific knowledge acquired on the $t=0$ audit to reduce his time inputs on the $t=1$ audit.

The following definitions are the same as in earlier models but, for convenience, are reproduced below:

w = the per unit time opportunity cost of auditors, assumed to be the same for all auditors over both time periods.

r = the discount rate, which is parametric and identical for all auditors and clients over both time periods.

$\pi^i(n,l)$ = the present value of the auditor's profit (total revenues minus total costs) over both time periods.

$\text{fee}_0(n)$ = the total audit fee at time zero when the client possesses no industry-level learning-by-doing advantages.

θ = the share of the time one premium which the incumbent auditor can capture, where $0 < \theta \leq 1$. Theta is parametric in the model and identical for all auditor-client pairs (and for both groups of clients).

For the clients in group two, in addition to firm-specific learning-by-doing advantages, there are also learning advantages at the industry level. Define γ as indexing industry level learning-by-doing advantages, where $0 < \gamma < 1$. The difference between firm-specific knowledge and industry knowledge is that the effect of α is to lower the $t=1$ auditor time input on one client, whereas the effect of γ is to lower the $t=1$ auditor time input on all clients within the industry group. We assume that the incumbent auditor is always the minimum cost producer of audit services for a given client, i.e., that

$$A_1(\alpha, \gamma) < A_1(\gamma).$$

If, in addition, we assume that perfect substitutes exist for all auditors (except for those with firm-specific knowledge), then auditors with industry experience will earn zero profits on new industry clients at time $t=1$.

The effects of the γ-parameter can be summarized as follows: first, it lowers the incumbent auditor's time inputs, and therefore total costs, on a given client's $t=1$ audit, i.e.,

$$A_1(\alpha, \gamma) < A_1(\alpha)$$

Second, while it also lowers this auditor's total costs on new industry clients at time one, the existence of perfect substitute auditors ensures that this auditor will earn (at most) zero profits on these clients. Third, it lowers the time inputs, and therefore total costs, of competitor auditors at time $t=1$, thereby lowering the alternative supply price at that time. In other words,

$$A_1(\gamma) < A_0.$$

With non-industry clients, the amount of the premium which the incumbent auditor can capture at time $t=1$ is θ times the alternative supply price at that time:

$$\theta[wA_0 - wA_1(\alpha)] = \theta w\alpha A_0.$$

With industry clients, the amount of the capturable premium to incumbent auditors is

$$\theta[wA_1(\gamma) - wA_1(\alpha,\gamma)] = \theta w[A_1(\gamma) - A_1(\alpha,\gamma)],$$

and the total $t=1$ audit fee which the incumbent auditor will charge for industry clients, fee_1^I, is

$$\text{fee}_1^I = \theta w[A_1(\gamma) - A_1(\alpha,\gamma)] + wA_1(\alpha,\gamma).$$

The incumbent auditor's fee at time one, fee_1^I, will exceed total costs at that time by $\theta w[A_1(\gamma) - A_1(\alpha,\gamma)]$. Competition among auditors at time zero will assure that $t=0$ audit fees are bid down to reflect an expected normal rate of return on industry and firm-specific knowledge. For clients within the industry group, define

$$\phi_R^I = \phi_R^I(l)$$

as the probability that the incumbent auditor is renewed by the client at time $t=1$. As in Chapter 5,

$$\phi_R = \phi_R(n)$$

is the probability of renewal of the incumbent auditor, for clients which possess no learning-by-doing advantages at the industry level. These two probabilities may differ across client groups in the current model, although $\phi_R(n)$ is assumed to be identical for clients within group one, while $\phi_R^I(l)$ is assumed to be identical for clients within group two.

The solution of the auditor's choice problem results in optimal values of the choice variables as functions of the contractual attributes:[5]

$$n = n^*(\alpha, \gamma, \theta)$$
$$l = l^*(\alpha, \gamma, \theta)$$

Therefore, through its functional dependence on n^* and l^*, the probability of retention of the incumbent auditor in the second period is also a function of the contractual attributes:

$$\phi_R = \phi_R(n^*(\alpha, \gamma, \theta))$$
$$\phi_R^I = \phi_R^I(l^*(\alpha, \gamma, \theta))$$

At time $t=0$, the audit fee for both industry and non-industry clients will adjust such that auditors earn an expected normal rate of return on all clients. The time zero audit fee will reflect the auditor incentives engendered by the contractual attributes. This functional dependence can be expressed as

$$\text{fee}_0 = \text{fee}_0(n^*(\alpha, \gamma, \theta))$$
$$\text{fee}_0^I = \text{fee}_0^I(l^*(\alpha, \gamma, \theta))$$

where $\text{fee}_0(n^*)$ is the optimal value of the time zero audit fee for non-industry clients, and $\text{fee}_0^I(l^*)$ is the optimal time zero audit fee for industry clients.[6]

At time $t=0$, auditors are asserted to maximize the present value of expected profits over both time periods by choosing

n = the total number of non-industry clients with two period time horizons, and

l = the total number of industry clients with two period time horizons.

Given the assumptions and definitions of the model, the auditor's decision problem can be expressed as:

$$\underset{n,l}{\text{maximize}} \ \pi^i(n,l) = n\{\text{fee}_0(n) - wA_0 + \frac{\phi_R(n)\,\theta w\, \alpha A_0}{(1+r)}\} - c^i(n)$$

$$+ l\{\text{fee}_0^I(l) - wA_0 + \frac{\phi_R^I(l)\,\theta w[A_1(\gamma) - A_1(\alpha,\gamma)]}{(1+r)}\} - c^i(l) \qquad (1)$$

Note that, by the assumptions of the model, the two decisions (choose n and choose l) are separable. The two first order conditions for maximization are

$$\pi_n^i = \text{fee}_0(n) - wA_0 + \frac{\phi_R(n)\theta w\, \alpha A_0}{(1+r)} - c_n^i + n\,\frac{\partial \text{fee}_0(n)}{\partial n}$$

$$+ [\frac{n\,\theta w\, \alpha A_0}{(1+r)}]\,\frac{\partial \phi_R(n)}{\partial n} = 0 \qquad (2)$$

$$\pi_I^i = \text{fee}_0^I(l) - wA_0 + \frac{\phi_R^I(l)\,\theta w\,[A_1(\gamma) - A_1(\alpha,\gamma)]}{(1+r)} - c_I^i$$

$$+ l\frac{\partial \text{fee}_0^I(l)}{\partial l} + \frac{l\theta w\,[A_1(\gamma) - A_1(\alpha,\gamma)]}{(1+r)}[\frac{\partial \phi_R^I(l)}{\partial l}] = 0. \qquad (3)$$

Equation (2) is the optimality condition that the auditor will increase n until the marginal costs equal the marginal benefits. Equation (3) is the optimality condition for l, the chosen number of industry clients. In addition, we assume that the second order conditions are satisfied. The sufficient second order conditions for this model are[7]

$$\pi_{nn}^i = 2\{\frac{\partial \text{fee}_0(n)}{\partial n} + [\frac{\theta w\,\alpha A_0}{(1+r)}]\frac{\partial \phi_R(n)}{\partial n}\} + n\frac{\partial^2 \text{fee}_0(n)}{\partial n^2}$$

$$+ [\frac{n\,\theta w\,\alpha A_0}{(1+r)}]\frac{\partial^2 \phi_R(n)}{\partial n^2} - c_{nn}^i < 0 \qquad (4)$$

$$\pi_{ll}^i = 2\{\frac{\partial \text{fee}_0^I(l)}{\partial l} + [\frac{\theta w[A_1(\gamma) - A_1(\alpha,\gamma)]}{(1+r)}]\frac{\partial \phi_R^I(l)}{\partial l}\}$$

$$+ l\frac{\partial^2 \text{fee}_0^I(l)}{\partial l^2} + \frac{l\theta w[A_1(\gamma) - A_1(\alpha,\gamma)]}{(1+r)}[\frac{\partial^2 \phi_R^I(l)}{\partial l^2}] - c_{ll}^i < 0 \qquad (5)$$

The simultaneous solution of equations (2) and (3) results in optimal values for the two choice variables:

$$n = n^*(\alpha, \gamma, \theta)$$
$$l = l^*(\alpha, \gamma, \theta)$$

Because the two choices are separable, i.e., because $\pi_{nl}^i = \pi_{ln}^i = 0$, and because perfect substitutes at time one exist for all auditors (except for those with firm-specific knowledge), the zero profit condition holds over the group of industry clients and over the group of non-industry clients. For clients within the industry group, the zero profit condition implies that

$$\text{fee}_0(l^*) = wA_0 - \frac{\phi_R^I(l^*)\,\theta w\,A_0(\alpha, \gamma)}{(1+r)} + \frac{c^i(l^*)}{l^*} \qquad (6)$$

Economies in Audit Technology

As can be seen by inspection of (6), there will be cross-sectional variation in fee$_0^i$ (l^*) as the costs of coordinating industry clients varies across auditors.

In general, auditors with differing $c^i(l)$ functions will choose different values for l^* and therefore charge differing audit fees at time zero. Symmetrically, auditors with differing $c^i(n)$ functions will choose different values for n^* and therefore charge different fee$_0(n^*)$. However, in this model, competition will ensure that all auditors expect to earn zero profits at equilibrium over both time periods combined (but not in each time period). Auditors will adjust their client holdings (and fee$_0(n^*)$ and fee$_0^i$ (l^*) will adjust) so that this condition holds.

The comparative statics predictions of the model emerge when we differentiate the first order conditions with respect to the contractual attributes. In this section, we are interested in how the optimal values of the choice variables change as industry-level learning-by-doing advantages change. Differentiating equations (2) and (3) with respect to γ yields the system of simultaneous equations:

$$\begin{bmatrix} \pi_{nn}^i & 0 \\ 0 & \pi_{ll}^i \end{bmatrix} \begin{bmatrix} \dfrac{\partial n^*}{\partial \gamma} \\ \dfrac{\partial l^*}{\partial \gamma} \end{bmatrix}$$

$$= \begin{bmatrix} 0 \\ \dfrac{-\theta w}{(1+r)} [\dfrac{\partial A_1(\gamma)}{\partial \gamma} - \dfrac{\partial A_1(\alpha,\gamma)}{\partial \gamma}] [\phi_R^l (l^*) + l^* \dfrac{\partial \phi_R^l (l^*)}{\partial \gamma}] \end{bmatrix} \quad (7)$$

Solving (7) using Cramer's rule yields

$$\dfrac{\partial n^*}{\partial \gamma} = 0 \quad (8)$$

and

$$\frac{\partial l^*}{\partial \gamma} = \frac{[\frac{-\theta w}{(1+r)}][\frac{\partial A_1(\gamma)}{\partial \gamma} - \frac{\partial A_1(\alpha,\gamma)}{\partial \gamma}][\phi_R^I(l^*) + l^* \frac{\partial \phi_R^I(l^*)}{\partial l}]}{\pi_{ll}^j} \qquad (9)$$

The denominator of (9) is negative by the sufficient second order condition. In the numerator, the first term in brackets,

$$[\frac{-\theta w}{(1+r)}],$$

is also negative.

The last term in brackets in the numerator,

$$[\phi_R^I(l^*) + l^* \frac{\partial \phi_R^I(l^*)}{\partial l}] = \frac{d}{dl}[l^* \phi_R^I(l^*)],$$

is the change in the expected number of two period industry clients as the chosen number of two period industry clients changes. With rational expectations, auditors will increase l^* only if $l^* \phi_R^I(l^*)$ increases as well, and thus the term

$$[\phi_R^I(l^*) + l^* \frac{\partial \phi_R^I(l^*)}{\partial l}]$$

is positive.

By the logic employed thus far, we can conclude that

$$\text{sign } \frac{\partial l^*}{\partial \gamma} = \text{sign }[\frac{\partial A_1(\gamma)}{\partial \gamma} - \frac{\partial A_1(\alpha,\gamma)}{\partial \gamma}]$$

In other words, whether subsequent to an increase in industry-level learning-by-doing advantages, an auditor has the incentive to increase the number of two period industry clients depends on whether $[\partial A_1(\gamma)/\partial \gamma - \partial A_1(\alpha,\gamma)/\partial \gamma$ is greater or less than zero. If the effect of the γ-increase is to lower this auditor's costs relative to the lowest cost alternative supplier, then $\partial l^*/\partial \gamma > 0$ and the incumbent auditor will have the incentive to increase the number of industry clients. If the effect of the γ-increase is to lower the competitors' costs relative to the incumbent's costs, then $\partial l^*/\partial \gamma < 0$ and the incumbent auditor will decrease the number of industry clients.

Whether $\partial l^*/\partial \gamma \gtreqless 0$ ultimately depends on the assumed relationship between firm-specific and industry-level learning-by-doing advantages. Suppose, for example, that γ-knowledge can only be used on other clients of the incumbent auditor, and the cost advantages of the incumbent auditor on this client are fully captured in the α-parameter. In this case, the incumbent auditor's time input is a function only of α,

$$A_1 = A_1(\alpha)$$

and $\partial A_1(\alpha)/\partial \gamma = 0$. Therefore the term $[\partial A_1(\gamma)/\partial \gamma - \partial A_1(\alpha)/\partial \gamma]$ is negative, which implies that $\partial l^*/\partial \gamma$ is negative as well. Intuitively, if the only effect of a γ-increase is to lower the alternative supply price at time $t=1$, auditors will choose to lower the number of two period industry clients chosen at time zero.

On the other hand, suppose that the relationship between α and γ is such that

$$A_1(\gamma) = (1-\gamma)A_0, \text{ and}$$
$$A_1(\alpha,\gamma) = (1-\gamma)(1+\alpha)A_0$$

The effect of γ in this case is to lower the costs of both the incumbent and his competitors at time one, relative to the costs of a new auditor with no industry experience at that time. The effect of α is to increase the effect of γ on the incumbent auditor. In other words, the α-parameter acts as a "multiplier" of the effect of the γ-parameter. As before

$$\text{sign} \frac{\partial l^*}{\partial \gamma} = \text{sign} [\frac{\partial A_1(\gamma)}{\partial \gamma} - \frac{\partial A_1(\alpha)}{\partial \gamma}]$$

In this special case,

$$\text{sign} \frac{\partial l^*}{\partial \gamma} = \text{sign } \alpha A_0$$

and

$$\frac{\partial l^*}{\partial \gamma} > 0$$

In this case, the effect of an increase in γ is to provide the incentive for the incumbent auditor to increase l^*. This result obtains because of the assumed relationship between γ-knowledge and α-knowledge, i.e., the nature of the assumed interrelationship of firm-specific and industry-level learning-by-doing advantages.

To summarize this section: we have developed a formal model of the auditor's choice of the number of industry and non-industry clients where

(1) all clients possess firm-specific learning-by-doing advantages, and

(2) some clients also possess industry-level learning-by-doing advantages, while others do not.

The model predicts that, as industry learning increases, whether auditors will increase or decrease the number of industry clients depends on the assumed relationship between firm-specific and industry-level learning-by-doing advantages. If the effect of increased industry learning is to increase the incumbent auditor's cost advantages relative to competitors, then he will have the incentive to increase I^*. If the effect of the parameter shift is to decrease the incumbent auditor's cost advantages measured relative to competitors, then he will have the incentive to decrease industry participation. In the following section, extant evidence concerning the degree of auditor specialization by client industry is reviewed.

6.3 Extant Evidence on Auditor Industry Specialization

Because the formal industry model yields no clear cut prediction about auditor specialization, extant evidence is reviewed in this section without an attempt to link it to the theory. This evidence must be treated as casual because of its limitation to the largest client firms only, and because of the lack of statistical tests (to determine whether the allocation of clients to auditors is significantly different from the one that would be expected if the allocation were random).

Several studies have attempted to analyze the client composition of large public accounting firms by classifying a sample of large client firms, both by auditor and by industry. Without exception, these studies have focused on the very largest industrial firms from the *Fortune Directory,* thereby potentially omitting a large number of firms in some industries. While large industrial firms may be of interest in their own right, it is difficult to generalize the findings of these studies because of the unknown bias introduced by omitting the (possibly large number of) smaller and medium-sized firms from a given industry group.

The first of the client composition studies was performed by Zeff and Fossum [1967]. Zeff and Fossum's sample consisted of firms listed in the *Fortune Directory* of August, 1965. They classified the sample into 38 industrial categories, based on *Standard & Poor's Industry Surveys* and auxiliary sources. Zeff and Fossum's findings were consistent with the

92   Economies in Audit Technology

hypothesis that large public accounting firms tend to specialize by client industry, although they performed no statistical tests to compare the allocation of clients which they observed with that expected if the allocation were random. Some of their more interesting findings are reproduced below:

> Price Waterhouse & Co. is the "leader" (where "leader" refers to a firm listed first in an industrial category where the second-place firm trails by 10 or more percentage points) in food products, machinery—industrial, meat and dairy products, office equipment, oil, rubber fabricating, and steel. Its position is especially strong in oil and steel, with 53 percent and 66 percent respectively.
>
> Haskins & Sells is the leader in autos, chemicals—industrial and household, and containers, while Lybrand, Ross Bros. & Montgomery is the leader in metals—aluminum, copper, fabricating; and telephone. Ernst & Ernst leads in auto parts; Arthur Andersen & Co. leads in utilities—gas; Peat, Marwick, Mitchell & Co. leads electronics—electrical; and Touche, Ross, Bailey & Smart leads in retail trade—department stores, mail orders, etc.
>
> In several industrial categories, two or three accounting firms are dominant, though no one firm may be said to lead. In tobacco, three firms account for 95 percent of the aggregate revenues, while in utilities—electric, three firms have 77 percent. Three firms account for 87 percent of aggregate revenues in railroads—trucking. In retail trade—chain, paper, and textiles—apparel, two firms account for more than 50 percent of aggregate revenues. In drugs, each of two firms has 23.6 percent of revenues. (pp. 305-6)

Zeff and Fossum caution the reader that it may be improper to draw inferences from some of their data because of the following classificatory problems:

(1)   In some industries, much activity is carried on by middle-sized and small companies, and the Zeff and Fossum sample consists entirely of large firms.

(2)   Firms are assigned to industrial categories based on their predominant activity. While they may be important producers in other industries, segment data was not publicly available in 1964.

These potential limitations also apply to the other studies reviewed in this section.

Rhode, Whitsell, and Kelsey [1974] replicated the Zeff and Fossum study on data from the May, 1972 *Fortune Directory*. Rhode, Whitsell, and Kelsey report that 70 firms, or 11.31% of the sample firms, had changed auditors between 1964 (the Zeff and Fossum study) and 1971 (their study). However, Rhode, Whitsell, and Kelsey only examined the two points in time; they did not examine data for these firms during the intervening period. Therefore, we can only conclude that at least 11.31% of the sample firms changed auditors over the time period 1964-1971.

Schiff and Fried [1976] replicated the Zeff and Fossum study on data from the 1973 *Fortune Directory*. Schiff and Fried's study is subject to the same industry classification problems as the earlier studies. Due to differences in classificatory schemes, as well as to changes in sample firms and industry classification over time, only twelve of the industry classifications were identical in Schiff and Fried, and Zeff and Fossum. An apparent contradiction exists between the Rhode, Whitsell, and Kelsey and the Schiff and Fried studies. As mentioned previously, Rhode, Whitsell, and Kelsey found that at least 70 firms had changed auditors in the period 1964-1971. Schiff and Fried compared the auditors of their sample with those of the Zeff and Fossum sample and concluded that at least 30 firms had changed auditors in the longer time period 1964-1973. While this discrepancy may be due to some clients switching back to auditors from which they had changed earlier, it appears that a more careful analysis of the intervening time period would be desirable.

Dopuch and Simunic [1979] replicated the Zeff and Fossum study on data from 1975 and attempted to compare the results from the two time periods. Dopuch and Simunic hypothesized that stable auditor market shares and limited auditor entry within industries may provide evidence of collusive arrangements among the large public accounting firms. They conclude that a comparison of their findings with those of Zeff and Fossum does not support this hypothesis. In particular, Dopuch and Simunic found that

> ... in 23 instances during the period, a Big Eight firm was a new entrant into a specific industry, and in 24 of the 32 industries, the dominant auditing firm in 1965 lost part of its market share during the next 10 years. (p. 9)

They concluded that auditor market shares do not appear to be stable over the time period 1965-1975, although again, no statistical tests were performed.

There are several problems with the Dopuch and Simunic conclusion. First, because they compute market shares as the percentage of total revenues in the industry, these shares will vary across time as total sales of client firms vary. Therefore, while auditor concentration measures may appear to change over time, they may in fact be quite stable; the appearance may be due to time series variation in client sales. Second, client firms may enter and leave the *Fortune Directory* over time, possibly creating the impression that a new auditor has entered the industry. In fact, what may have occurred is that a client firm has been listed in the *Fortune Directory* for the first time. Thus, Dopuch and Simunic's statement that "in 23 instances during the period, a Big Eight firm was a new entrant into a specific industry" is suspect. These potential problems with the Dopuch and Simunic analysis would tend to bias the results toward finding fluctuating market shares when in fact they were stable.

Coe and Palmon [1979] attempt to ascertain whether firms in industries which have higher measures of auditor concentration change auditors more or less frequently than do other firms. They define auditor industry (COMPU-

STAT two-digit classification) concentration as the number of auditors in an industry divided by the number of sample companies in that industry. They divide their sample into a high concentration group (ranks 1-15 by auditor concentration) and a low concentration group (ranks 16-30). Coe and Palmon's results are:

> Using T-Test for groups, the null hypothesis that the difference in the mean value of auditor turnover between the high concentration group and the low concentration group is zero is rejected (α = .024) in favor of the hypothesis that a higher turnover exists in high concentration industries. (p. 10)

There are several problems with the Coe and Palmon study. First, the COMPUSTAT two-digit classification scheme is unlikely to be a meaningful measure of an industry. Second, Coe and Palmon's auditor concentration measure is subject to fluctuation when client firms are listed and delisted from the COMPUSTAT tapes,[8] although it is not weighted by client sales (as was the measure used by Dopuch and Simunic). Contrary to the conclusion of Dopuch and Simunic, Coe and Palmon find that auditor industry concentration is increasing over time (in the time period 1952-1975). Thus, the results of these two studies appear to be contradictory and a more careful analysis is in order before conclusions about the behavior of auditor industry concentration over time can be properly drawn.

To summarize this chapter: we first examined reasons for the existence of industry learning advantages. These reasons include operational and organizational similarities within a client industry group, the existence of industry-specific accounting and/or auditing standards, and regulation by client industry. Two potential countervailing forces are the existence of benefits to client diversification and confidentiality costs. A formal model of the auditor's choice of the number of industry and non-industry clients was presented. When industry-level learning-by-doing advantages increase, the model predicts that auditors will increase the number of two period industry clients only if their cost advantages have increased relative to competitors. Finally, extant evidence on the extent of auditor specialization by client industry was presented in the final section of the chapter. In the following chapter, conclusions and some possible avenues for future research are presented.

7

Conclusions

This chapter enumerates the major conclusions of this study in their order of presentation. Suggestions for future theoretical extensions and empirical tests of the theory are also provided. Because formal models are stylized representations of real world phenomena, simplifying assumptions are necessary. Whether the assumptions of the current models are appropriate ultimately rest on the empirical validity of their predictions. Perhaps future research will shed light on this issue.

Extant audit research has claimed that audit services are a public good and that the output of the audit process is unobservable. Contrary to these claims, the analysis in Chapter 3 concluded that audit services demanded as a monitoring device possess significant private-good aspects. To the extent that the firm's investment in audit services results in more efficient operations, efficient capital markets will ensure that current owners are compensated by increased valuation of the firm. Furthermore, intra-shareholder free rider problems are effectively prevented by extant corporate structure, because joint ownership combined with proportional sharing is sufficient to remove externalities.

With regard to the second assertion, that audit output is unobservable: we concluded that this assertion is erroneous because no audits would be demanded if it were true. If audit output were unobservable, i.e., infinitely costly to observe, then clients would not contract with auditors because it would not be possible to ascertain at any finite cost whether they were receiving the audit services for which they had contracted. Therefore, we concluded that, while audit quality may be costly for consumers to evaluate, it cannot be unobservable.

When observation of product quality is costly, alternative market arrangements may arise which enable some other (less costly to observe) variable to serve as a surrogate for quality. If auditing confers benefits that are sufficiently important to individuals, then they will have the incentive to devise arrangements which enable them to capture these benefits. One possible arrangement is for the auditor's brand name to signal the quality of audit services to consumers; other possible arrangements are collateral bonding, institutional arrangements, and advertising. Because these arrangements are, to some extent, substitutes for each other, one potential area for future research is to develop a theory which specifies the conditions under which one (or another) arrangement is more likely to be observed.

For example, auditors with established brand names may be less likely to benefit from the lifting of the professional ban on advertising than are other auditors. Therefore, a testable implication might be that, subsequent to removal of the ban on advertising, "brand name" auditors are relatively less likely to advertise than are other audit firms. Or, prior to the lifting of the ban, one could attempt to ascertain whether "brand name" auditors were more opposed to its removal than were other auditors.

Because of the long-standing professional ban on advertising (now removed), the nature of the auditor's brand name capital investment is likely to differ from that of, say, manufacturing firms. In either case, building a reputation is a costly process. A theory of the process by which auditors establish brand names is another potential area for future research. The auditor's investments in brand name capital should satisfy several criteria: they should be readily observable, firm-specific, and preferably have a low salvage value should the auditor opportunistically lower audit quality.

We concluded in Chapter 5 that one investment which satisfies these criteria is the auditor's investments in specialized assets. Recall that specialized assets refers to the value of the future economic profit which an auditor can capture due to specialized knowledge of client operations and/or positive transactions costs of changing auditors. While the auditor's specialized assets on one client serve to impair auditor independence with respect to that particular client, his specialized assets on all clients serves as a sort of collateral bond which constrains auditor opportunism.

Specialized assets, i.e., future economic profit from a relationship with a given client, arise in our model because of the existence of learning-by-doing advantages and positive transactions costs of changing auditors. The existence of these factors, even in a competitive market for audit services, implies that the contracting parties will be locked into a bilateral monopoly position at the recontracting interval. As long as the auditor possesses some relative bargaining power, this condition implies that he will charge a fee in future periods which exceeds total costs in those periods. The existence of future economic profit is presumed, both by regulators and by the accounting profession, to impair auditor independence.

Regulators and the profession have also asserted that "low-balling" on the initial audit engagement impairs auditor independence by creating future economic interest in clients. We show, in Chapter 4, that this assertion is erroneous; "low-balling" itself does not impair independence. Rather, it is the existence of specialized assets which creates future economic interest. We concluded that "low-balling" is a competitive response which should not itself be of concern to regulators and the profession. Because the Chapter 4 model predicts that "low-balling" will increase subsequent to an increase in the transactions costs of changing auditors, we also concluded that regulation which increases these costs (ASR-165 et. al.) is inconsistent with regulation which attempts to curtail "low-balling" (ASR-250).

In Chapter 5, we develop a theory which potentially explains why client firms change auditors. Intuitively, because of the existence of specialized assets, choosing a long term relationship with an auditor economizes on audit fees. On the other hand, long term relationships pose independence problems not present in short term contracting. Our model asserts that the length of the auditor-client relationship is determined by trading off these two factors. While this simple tradeoff cannot capture all relevant considerations in every case, it is consistent with "conventional wisdom" in the auditing literature.

Furthermore, the theory generates two predictions which are potentially refutable. Specifically, this model predicts that the average length of the auditor-client relationship will increase when, ceteris paribus,

(1) the transactions costs of changing auditors increase, or

(2) learning-by-doing advantages increase.

Empirical tests of these two hypotheses are a logical extension of the current research.

The Chapter 5 model also generates testable implications about changes in auditor concentration over time. Specifically, the model predicts that the average number of clients per auditor will increase (and the number of auditors decrease) when, ceteris paribus,

(1) the transactions costs of changing auditors increase, or

(2) learning-by-doing advantages increase.

In other words an increase in the value of specialized assets implies that, ceteris paribus, auditor concentration will increase and clients will increasingly choose longer term relationships with auditors. These implications are potentially testable, and tests of them would also appear to be promising areas for future research.

The model developed in Chapter 6 allows industry knowledge, as well as general and firm-specific knowledge on the part of auditors. It is less complete than earlier models, and does not offer an unambiguous prediction. Therefore, further theoretical development needs to be done before refutable implications emerge. Specifically, the relationship between firm-specific and industry-level learning-by-doing needs to be more carefully specified. While the existence of industry learning allows a given auditor to lower his total costs on other industry clients, it simultaneously allows his competitors to lower their costs as well. Whether a given auditor is "better off" after a parameter shift which has the effect of increasing industry learning advantages depends on whether the change has improved his position relative to his competitors, or has improved their position relative to him. Which of these obtains depends, in turn, on the nature of the assumed relationship between firm-specific and industry-level learning advantages.

Future theoretical development would isolate particular industries in which one or the other type of knowledge is expected to be relatively more important. In other words, in some industries the marginal benefits of increased industry learning advantages can be expected to outweigh the marginal costs (and vice versa). Identification of such industries could lead to potentially refutable predictions about cross-sectional variation in auditor industry concentration. Without further specification of the interrelationship between firm-specific and industry knowledge, no testable implications are forthcoming.

Extant empirical research dealing with auditor industry specialization is limited at best (see the literature review in Section 6.3). No currently published study presents statistical tests, for example, of whether the allocation of clients to auditors within industries differs from that expected if the allocation were random. And yet, this area appears to be a particularly fruitful one when one considers the Metcalf Subcommittee's allegations (and potential anti-trust implications for auditors). Both auditor industry concentration and auditor concentration in the broader market for audit services are important research topics for these reasons.

In conclusion, this study represents an attempt to apply economic analysis to understand the structure of the auditor-client contractual relationship. As such, it is a broad endeavor which provides insight into some of the basic contractual attributes in this relationship. Perhaps even more importantly, it uncovers issues and problem areas which merit further attention. The purpose of this final chapter was to identify some of these areas, in which future research efforts may prove fruitful, not only to academics, but to regulators and practicing accountants as well.

Appendix A

Requirements for Membership in the AICPA: SEC Practice and Private Companies Practice Sections

		SEC Practice Section	Private Companies Practice Section
(1)	Mandatory peer review every three years	Yes	Yes
(2)	Public Oversight Board	Yes	Not Required
(3)	Individual AICPA membership	All partners, shareholders and proprietors resident in the U.S. who are qualified for membership in the AICPA must be members of the AICPA	All partners, shareholders and proprietors must be (1) CPAs (2) Members of the AICPA
(4)	Adhere to quality control standards	Yes	Yes
(5)	40 hours of annual continuing education	Yes	Yes
(6)	Mandatory audit partner rotation every 5 years	Yes	No
(7)	Mandatory review of audit report by a partner other than the partner in charge of the audit	Yes	No
(8)	File certain publicly available information such as (a) The number and names of SEC clients for which the firm is principal auditor and	Yes	No

Appendix A

	SEC Practice Section	Private Companies Practice Section
any changes in clients (b) The number of SEC audit clients each of whose total domestic fees exceed 5% of total domestic firm fees and the percentage that these firms represent (c) Gross fees for accounting and auditing, tax and MAS expressed as a percentage of total gross fees		
(9) Maintain prescribed liability insurance	Yes	Yes
(10) Refrain from certain management advisory services	Yes	No
(11) Report annually to the audit committee or the board of directors on MAS provided to SEC clients	Yes	No
(12) Report to the audit committee or board of directors on the nature of disagreements with management on financial accounting and reporting matters and auditing procedures which, if not satisfactorily resolved, would have caused the issuance of a qualified opinion	Yes	No
(13) Authority to impose sanctions on member firms: (a) Require corrective measures including with respect to individuals	Yes	Yes

SEC Practice Section	Private Companies Practice Section
(b) Additional requirements for continuing education (c) Special peer reviews (d) Admonishments, censures, or reprimands (e) Monetary fines (f) Suspension (g) Expulsion	

Appendix B

the time horizon alone is not sufficient to assure that $fee_0 = wA_0$; rather, the existence of costless contracting is both necessary and sufficient.

---

* If the zero profit condition is satisfied, then the present value of the total audit fees is constrained to be less than or equal to the present value of the total audit fees from hiring two non-colluding auditors to compete in every period. Assuming the costs of preventing collusion are zero, this condition is that

$$wA_0 - \varepsilon_0 + \sum_{t=1}^{n} \frac{wA + \varepsilon}{(1+r)^t} \leq wA_0 + \frac{w(A_0 - A)}{(1+r)} + \sum_{t=1}^{n} \frac{wA}{(1+r)^t}$$

$$-\varepsilon_0 + \sum_{t=1}^{n} \frac{\varepsilon}{(1+r)^t} \leq \frac{w(A_0 - A)}{(1+r)}$$

which is satisfied when

$$-\varepsilon_0 + \sum_{t=1}^{n} \frac{\varepsilon}{(1+r)^t} = 0 \qquad \text{(zero profit condition)}$$

as long as $w(A_0 - A) > 0$, which is true by assumption.

Appendix C

Summary of Regulation Governing Changes of Auditor

(1) **Securities Release #34-9344** (effective for Form 8-K on or after 10/31/71)
   Text: If there has been a change in principal accountant, state the date when the new accountant was engaged. Furnish a separate letter stating whether (in the prior 18 months) there were any disagreements with the former accountant on any matter of accounting principles or practices, financial statement disclosure, or auditing procedure, which disagreements if not resolved to the satisfaction of the former accountant would have caused him to make reference in connection with his opinion to the subject matter of the disagreement. The registrant shall also request the former principal accountant to state in a letter whether he agrees and, if not, stating the respects in which he does not. The registrant shall furnish this letter to the Commission along with his own.

(2) **ASR-165** (effective for Form 8-K and proxy statements after 1/31/75 and for financial statements for periods beginning on or after 1/1/75).
   Form 8-K Amendment: The resignation of the former accountant (as well as the engagement of a new accountant) is a reportable event. Changes in the accountant for a significant subsidiary on whom the principal accountant expressed reliance becomes a reportable event. The period covered is extended from 18 months to the two most recent fiscal years and any subsequent interim period. All disagreements at the decision making level are covered, whether resolved or not. The registrant must state whether, for the past two years, the principal accountant's report contained an adverse opinion or a disclaimer of opinion or was qualified as to uncertainty, audit scope, or accounting principles. The response of the former accountant shall be filed as an Exhibit attached to the 8-K.
   Financial Statement Disclosure: Requirement is disclosure in a note to the financial statements of any material disagreement on any matter of accounting principles or practices (as disclosed in Form 8-K within 24 months). Footnote disclosure is also required of any transactions or events occurring during the fiscal year in which the change of accountants took

place or during the subsequent fiscal year which are similar to any which gave rise to a reported disagreement and which are differently accounted for.

Proxy Statements: Similar to Form 8-K, the disagreement is disclosed, and the former accountant may include a brief statement expressing his views. In addition, the proxy statement will state whether or not the present and former accountants will be available at the annual meeting to express their views and to answer questions.

(3) **ASR-194:** (effective for financial statements filed after 8/31/76)
Text: ASR-165 required disclosure in a note to the financial statements of both (1) the fact of, and (2) the effect on the financial statements of a reported disagreement. ASR-194 amends this requirement by mandating (1) only in the presence of (2). ASR-194 mitigates the requirements under ASR-165.

(4) **ARS-247** (effective for Forms 8-K and proxy materials filed after 7/31/78)
Text: ASR-247 requires that firms disclose whether or not the Board of Directors or Audit Committee has approved any change in auditors.

Appendix D

The Use of Engagement Letters to Formalize Auditor-Client Contracts

As discussed in Chapter 5, the contract which usually serves as a written record of the auditor-client ex ante agreement is the engagement letter. Not all public accounting firms use engagement letters, nor do firms which use them employ them for all clients. For example, a 1972 survey of 215 public accounting firms in the State of Ohio (Yocum [1972]) reports that most of the respondents relied on informal, rather than on explicit agreements:

> ... 63 percent of the firms "generally do not use an engagement letter," and only 7 percent "always" use such a letter. Deviations from this State-average pattern were not significant by Chapter areas, but were substantial by size of firm and by predominant type of business. Among the intermediate ($150,001-$250,000 gross revenue) and largest-sized (over $750,000) firms the engagement letter is "usually" used by 48 and 33 percent of the firms, respectively, and "always" used by 12 and 41.7 percent respectively (compared to 30 percent, "usually," and 7 percent, "always," for all firms). Again, it would appear, though, that the differences in usages are associated primarily with the predominant type of business for the firm: 78 percent of the firms predominantly involved in "Opinion Audit" and 41 percent of the firms predominantly involved in "Tax Service" work "always" or "usually" use an engagement letter, while only 14 percent of the firms in "Writeup Work" predominantly "usually" use the letter (no firms use it "always"). (pp. 39-41)

Thus it appears that larger accounting firms and those predominantly involved in auditing financial statements are relatively more likely to negotiate explicit contracts with their clients. In addition, it is likely that the percent of total revenues from auditing increases with the size of the public accounting firm. If this is the case, then the two factors are reinforcing, and the larger the audit firm, the more likely the use of explicit contracts.

The use of engagement letters has also likely increased in recent years due to increases in auditors' legal liability. A landmark case in this area is *1136 Tenants' Corporation vs. Max Rothenberg & Company,* which was finally decided in 1972. In this case, there was no written record of the agreement between auditor and client. The auditor claimed that he had been engaged only to do "write up work," and not to perform an audit. The client alleged that the auditor had been engaged to perform an audit. The court found for the plaintiff. According to Guy and Winters [1972],

> The *1136 Tenants'* decision (involving a $237,278.83 judgment relative to a $600 annual fee) has pointed out the need for an engagement letter identifying the nature of services to be performed by the accountant. (p. 47)

Extant empirical evidence supports the prediction that one effect of an increase in auditors' legal liability is an increased use of engagement letters. Bedingfield [1974] sent a questionnaire to partners of both national and non-national auditing firms in an attempt to ascertain the profession's response to the increase in auditors' legal liability. Thirty-two percent of the respondents indicated that their firm had extended audit procedures in general. One example given by respondents was the use of engagement letters on all audits. Guy and Winters [1972] queried public accounting firms in Texas about their policies for the use of engagement letters for clients requesting unaudited financial statements. Guy and Winters' results were that, of their sample, 11% reported that they always used engagement letters, 41% said they did sometimes, and 48% said that they never did. Guy and Winters attempted to correlate the use of engagement letters for unaudited financial statements with the respondents' knowledge of the *1136 Tenants' Case.* They reported that "thirty-five percent of the practitioners who were familiar with the case (very or somewhat) replied that their knowledge of the case resulted in a change in their engagement letter policy" (p. 49).

The format and content of the engagement letter, if used, apparently varies among auditors and across engagements. An engagement letter may delineate the scope of the engagement, the responsibilities of auditor and client personnel, the auditor's fee arrangements, etc. According to the AICPA publication, *Sample Engagement Letters for an Accounting Practice,* the items which are normally included in the engagement letter are:

    a. Name of entity and its year end.
    b. Statement(s) to be examined or prepared.
    c. Scope of services, including limitations imposed by client.
    d. Type of opinion, disclaimer or other report to be rendered.
    e. Disclaimer of responsibility for detecting fraud.
    f. Obligations of the client's staff to prepare schedules and statements.
    g. Requirement that accountant approve all printed material his report appears in.
    h. Responsibility for preparation or review of tax returns and subsequent tax examinations.

i. Fee or method of determining fee.
j. Frequency of billing and client's obligations for payment, including retainer if applicable.
k. Provision for client's acceptance signature and date.
l. Expression of thanks for being selected as auditors or to perform other services.
m. In new engagements, the client should take the responsibility for getting the cooperation of the prior accountant.

To summarize: in this appendix we discussed evidence that the use of engagement letters to formalize the auditor-client relationship is by no means universal. This evidence suggests that larger public accounting firms and those predominantly supplying audit services are relatively more likely to employ engagement letters. In addition, it appears that the use of engagement letters has increased in recent years due perhaps to greater auditor legal liability.

Notes

Chapter 1

1. See, for example, Alchian and Demsetz [1972], Jensen and Meckling [1976], and Fama [1980].

2. Opportunism is defined as self-seeking with deceit and includes such behavior as fraud, lying, misrepresentation, etc. In order for opportunism to occur, it must be costly for one party to observe the other party's behavior.

3. Other papers which can be included under this rubric include Watts [1977], Watts and Zimmerman [March 1979, July 1979], Benston [1979], and Ng [1978].

4. For a different formulation of the "low balling" phenomenon and a more extensive discussion of the implications for disclosure regulations, see DeAngelo [August 1981].

5. For a more extensive development of the link between auditor size and audit quality, see DeAngelo [December 1981].

6. See, for example, Burton and Roberts [1976], Carpenter and Strawser [1971], Barlev and Benston [1974], Coe and Palmon [1979], Wallace [1979], Bolten and Crockett [1979], and Fried and Schiff [1979].

7. See, for example, Zeff and Fossum [1967], Rhode, Whitsell, and Kelsey [1974], Schiff and Fried [1976], and Dopuch and Simunic [1979].

8. See, for example, Ng [1978], Barefield and Beck [1979], Magee [1979], and Dopuch and Simunic [1979].

9. In addition to Ng [1978], Barefield and Beck [1979], Magee [1979], and Dopuch and Simunic [1979], see Kaplan [1978].

Chapter 2

1. With costly contracting, the original owners will be unable to capture 100% of these potential benefits, as they would if contracting were costless.

2. Ibid.

3. Ronen [1979] makes a similar argument by asserting the dual function of accounting to be:

> "(1) A means of monitoring for owners of the corporation to guarantee the safeguarding, and effective management of the owners' assets entrusted to agents (management), and
> (2) A means of informing stockholders and potential investors about the prospects of investing in the corporation." (p. 416)

The distinction between auditing and accounting is not a clear one because the commodity being produced is "audited financial statements." These two general categories comprise the "stewardship" demand for audited financial statements. Benston [1979] argues that other demanders may exist, e.g., government agencies, consumers of the firm's products, and consumer "watchdogs." We confine our analysis to the two categories specified above.

4. This statement is true only when perfect substitutes exist for agents, i.e., when competitive labor markets ensure that agents earn zero economic rents at equilibrium.

5. The term, original owners, is used interchangeably with the term, "current shareholders of the firm."

6. Watts and Zimmerman [March 1979, July 1979] discuss the historical evolution of auditing. Prior to the 1880's, shareholders typically appointed one of their group to examine the firm's books on their behalf. This person could engage a professional accountant to assist in the examination. Eventually the accountant came to replace the shareholder as outside auditor.

7. This role of auditing is analytically identical to the function of the brand name mechanism. Independent verification of the firm's financial statements by a professional auditor whose reputation is at stake is similar to, say, the independent assessment of a consumer durable in *Consumer Reports* or the rating of a bond issue by Moody's or Standard & Poor's.

8. This compensation will take the form of a higher price for the firm's bonds. To the extent that potential shareholders delegate decision-making authority to professional managers, they may also demand assurance about future firm decisions (from management). For example, corporate charters and bylaws may retain shareholder rights to certain decisions by requiring shareholder approval of mergers, appointment of auditors, etc.

9. See Jensen and Meckling [1976], Smith and Warner [1979], and Fama and Miller [1972] for elaboration of shareholder strategies for expropriating bondholders.

10. See Smith and Warner [1979] for a detailed descriptive analysis of bond covenants.

11. The logic which follows is largely based on reasoning which can be found in Barzel [1977, 1979]. My debt to Professor Barzel should be obvious.

12. Manufacturers will voluntarily shelf-date milk cartons if the increased price they get (minus what they now lose in spoilage) for milk times the quantity sold exceeds the cost of providing this information. In the absence of mandated shelf-dating, manufacturers of

non-fresh milk will "lose" to the extent that the milk of those manufacturers which disclose no information will be "priced out" by consumers to reflect the joint probability that the milk is fresh and is not voluntarily shelf-dated. With mandated shelf-dating, manufacturers of non-fresh milk will also incur costs of disclosing that their milk is not fresh.

13. Unless it is costless to detect auditor fraud, we cannot be certain that voluntary disclosers are high quality firms.

14. If there is nothing "unique" about the project, i.e., if it is a zero net present value investment with optimal contracting, then the economic rents to ownership are zero. This will be true to the extent that perfect substitutes exist for the investment project. In order to illustrate how the rents are distributed, if present, we continue to assume a positive net present value investment opportunity.

15. We have assumed that competition in the labor markets is sufficient to preclude managers from earning economic rents. To the extent that the labor market is not efficient (an empirical issue), managers effectively "own" the property rights to some portion of the firm's productive opportunity.

16. As in footnote 15, Chapter 2, concerning the labor market, to the extent that the capital market is not sufficiently competitive to remove economic rents to new shareholders and bondholders, these individuals will also effectively "own" the property rights to some portion of the firm's productive opportunity.

17. This argument relies on information and firm securities being jointly supplied, i.e., information is "tied in" to firm ownership. This argument is virtually identical to that presented in Demsetz [1970]. To the extent that information use is not effectively tied in to firm ownership, free rider problems may develop. For example, it is often argued that investors who use audited financial statements to sort firms are free-riding on the information of firms who securities they do not subsequently purchase. However, if losses of this type were material to firms, it would be worth their while to charge a fee for financial statements (much as newspapers charge a fee for the information which they supply). Because we do not observe firms charging a separate fee for financial statements in the absence of disclosure regulation, we can infer that the expected costs of excluding free riders exceed these losses.

Chapter 3

1. Consumers of audit services include current and potential owners (both shareholders and bondholders), managers, consumers of the firm's products, employees, government agencies, etc.

2. The well-known problem with a public good is that of determining the "correct" amount of the good to produce. As Alchian and Allen [1972] describe it, "potential users of new public goods are tempted to conceal their valuations so someone else can be inveigled into paying, then those who do not pay can, once the good is produced, use all that is available without having borne its production costs" (pp. 147-48).

3. Increased firm efficiency is an attribute which is valued in the capital market, whether the source of the increased efficiency is an audit or, say, a technological improvement.

4. This statement assumes that shareholders view the only benefit of an audit as an increase in wealth, i.e., that shareholders do not get consumption from auditing directly, but only through increases in firm value. This assumption is the traditional one made in the theory of the firm when evaluating firm investment/financing decisions.

5. See Demsetz [1970] for a more complete discussion of how tying in a public good to another commodity which is private may remove the potential free rider problem.

6. Current shareholders both pay for and enjoy the value increment due to auditing in proportion to their invested wealth in the firm: therefore relative ownership shares remain the same after the firm contracts for auditing services, and no intra-stockholder wealth transfers are effected.

7. As a practical matter, the ex ante calculation of the increase in expected future cash flows may be more difficult to calculate for the purchase of audit services than for the purchase of, say, a machine. The potential difficulty in cash flow computation does not alter the conceptual result that auditing possesses significant private good aspects.

8. This characterization of audit quality differs slightly from Ng's characterizations as the probability of detection of a material error. Our definition of audit quality is the user-assessed probability that the auditor will both discover and report a given error. This latter definition is also used by Watts and Zimmerman [July 1979].

9. Several strategies are available to market participants who wish to evaluate audit quality directly. These include: hiring two noncolluding auditors, probability elicitation techniques, observation of audit failures (a joint product of auditor and client actions) with a time lag, etc. All of these strategies are likely to be costly, but not infinitely costly to implement. For example, waiting for audit failures to reveal themselves has a (time) cost.

10. These consumers include current and potential clients, investors, government agencies, consumers, managers, shareholders and bondholders, potential investors, and other third party users.

11. The brand name phenomenon is only one of many possible arrangements which may economize on the costs of quality determination. Another potential arrangement is a collateral or performance bond (see Chapter 3, footnote 20). Additionally, the evaluation of quality may be performed by government, or by a professional body. Finally, as discussed in Chapter 5 and elaborated in DeAngelo [December 1981], auditor size also serves a quality-guaranteeing function.

12. Darby and Karni [1973] call goods which exhibit this property "credence goods." Examples of credence goods include medical and automobile repair services.

13. According to the Cohen Commission Report, "A research study for the Commission and extensive discussions with users indicate that users consider the name and reputation of the public accounting firm to be their principal source of information about the quality of the audit. . . . Users of the financial statements presently have no knowledge of the quality of the financial information, the accounting and control systems that are the principal source of the information, or the price-setting arrangements made for the audit. Similar to users of many consumer products, the user of financial statements is left with little other than the "brand name" or the name and reputation of the public accounting firm as a

Notes for Chapter 3   117

basis for judging quality'' (p. 111). See Klein, Crawford, and Alchian [1978], and Klein and Leffler [forthcoming] for discussion of the use of price as a signal where product quality is uncertain.

14. There are obviously other factors influencing such switches; for example, "Big Eight" firms may have more expertise in auditing large clients, overseeing the proparation of SEC documents, etc.

15. Another surrogate for audit output is auditor input. Alchian and Demsetz [1972] provide a comprehensive discussion of the role of monitoring inputs in team production. The audit process can be viewed as a joint production process with auditor and client inputs. The more production function is known, the better do inputs surrogate output. However, while observation of auditor time inputs may be relatively easy for clients, it is not likely to be so for capital market participants. In addition, one problem with surrogates in general as Barzel [1979] notes, is that individuals optimize with respect to the surrogate, not with respect to the underlying variable. For example, when auditors are paid by, say, the hour, they will have the incentive to maximize auditor time inputs, not audit output. The extent to which they can do this is, of course, governed by competition in the market for audit services.

16. Presumably, the social costs of audit failure are perceived to be sufficiently high for the government (and the accounting profession) to intervene. Since it is also costly for regulators and the profession to observe the quality of a given audit opinion, they choose to constrain the surrogate, auditor input. Standardization of auditor input may also serve other functions: first, it may provide a defense to the auditor in litigation. Second, standardization may also economize on contracting costs, much in the same way as do "boiler plates" in standardized contracts.

17. This organizational form may also be the one which enables the least-cost monitoring of partners' activities. See Alchian and Demsetz [1972] for a discussion of how professional partnerships may economize on monitoring costs.

18. Furthermore, this statement also assumes that financial statements are exogenous, i.e., independent of the incentive effects of the presence of an auditor on management's decisions.

19. Another possible arrangement to enforce audit quality is for the auditor to purchase insurance. See Mayers and Smith [1979] for a positive theory of insurance.

20. Edwards [1960] documents the use of a collateral bond for the exchange of audit services in the brief time period 1920-1923. During this period, the National Association of Certified Public Accountants was privately incorporated. This organization collected a fee and dues, administered examinations and maintained a bond to "protect the members of this organization from suits brought against them for negligence in the fulfillment of their duties" (p. 119). Suits by the government against the issuance of certificates by the National Association established states' rights to certify public accountants.

21. Clients may, however, extract payment from the auditor by threatening to claim the auditor cheated. This incentive to "hold up" the auditor is the same for both the brand name and the collateral bond arrangements. In addition, with the collateral bond arrangement, clients also can capture direct economic benefits from actually claiming auditor cheating.

While a collateral bond forfeitable to a third party would circumvent this problem, it may also provide undesirable incentives for clients and third parties to collude against the auditor.

22. Unlike the enforcement of minimum audit standards by the courts (an exogenous party to the contract), the enforcement mechanism used here is an implicit contractual agreement that clients will terminate an auditor who "cheats" on quality. Client termination, in turn, imposes a capital loss (of future audit fees) on auditors.

23. See Klein, Crawford, and Alchian [1978] and Klein and Leffler [forthcoming] for a more extensive discussion of last period problems.

Chapter 4

1. This analysis does not imply that the audit opinion will have no value unless the auditor always tells the truth. Rather, the greater the incentive for the auditor to tell the truth, the greater the value of the auditor's opinion.

2. These costs will include the present value of the loss in future audit fees resulting from the loss of reputation, should the auditor be caught "cheating" and the probability of being caught.

3. This statement presumes that the auditor is able to capture at least some of these benefits, i.e., that he possesses some "bargaining power" vis à vis the client.

4. Costless contracting at time zero for all future periods would enable auditors and clients to contract away all future economic interest by an appropriate lump sum payment at time zero. Costless contracting results are neither very interesting, nor very realistic. In all the models which follow, contracting among individuals is assumed to be a costly process.

5. While generally accepted auditing standards mandate that successor and predecessor auditors confer, auditors do not generally exchange working papers, train their replacements, etc. In other words, once an auditor is terminated, the value of his specialized knowledge essentially falls to zero.

6. Modeling the audit process as a joint one only serves to complicate the analysis without altering the qualitative predictions of the model.

7. We assume that last period contracts are perfectly enforceable in order to assure that auditors will supply the services for which they contract at $t=1$. Otherwise, last period problems may cause the solution to unravel (see Chapter 3).

8. This formulation implicitly assumes that auditor knowledge can be partitioned into two mutually exclusive and exhaustive subsets:

    (1) general knowledge applicable in auditing all potential clients, and

    (2) specialized knowledge applicable to auditing one particular client.

In actuality, a third type of knowledge is likely to be important in the exchange of audit services: industry-specific knowledge. Industry-specific knowledge is the subject of Chapter 6.

9. Note, however, that removal of the bilateral monopoly (and related independence problems) in future periods is not costlessly achieved. Rather, the costs of circumventing the problem are constrained to be less than or equal to the costs of training a second (non-colluding) auditor to compete in each future period. These costs would also include the costs of preventing collusion, if preventing collusion is costly.

10. See Appendix B for a deterministic formulation of the auditor's multi-period decision problem in an infinite time horizon model.

11. In this simple model ϕ_R is not a function of θ because θ does not affect the present value of total audit fees paid in both periods; it only affects whether they are paid at $t=0$ or $t=1$. Furthermore, θ is assumed to be identical for all auditors. In the next chapter, the quality of audit services is shown to rely on θ, i.e., θ affects the value of audit services to the client. In this chapter, audit quality is fixed and thus $\partial \phi_R / \partial \theta = 0$.

12. Under perfect competition with no fixed start-up costs, both $\pi_0^* = 0$ and $E(\pi_1^*) = 0$ as well, because no learning-by-doing advantages can be captured by the incumbent auditor at time one. This characterization of competition implies no future economic interest in the client and hence, no independence problem. It also implies the absence of brand name capital investments upon which auditors earn income in future periods.

13. We shall see in the next chapter that the existence of economic profits in future periods has a negative impact on client firm value. Therefore auditors and clients have the incentive to contract for the audit fee structure which most closely approximates the perfectly competitive (with no fixed costs) fee structure. Since contracting is not costless, this fee structure will generally not be the least-cost solution. The current model ignores valuation issues in order to concentrate on the "low-balling" phenomenon.

14. To the extent that imperfect competition among auditors enables auditors to earn economic rents, auditor and client can be expected to share in any monopoly profits from auditing. In the absence of significant barriers to entry, positive economic profits to auditors would not be expected to persist in long run equilibrium.

Chapter 5

1. This choice is necessarily a simplified one, because it is a model of reality, rather than reality itself. Therefore there is, as with all models, the possibility that significant explanatory variables have been omitted from the analysis. Whether the model is an appropriate one or not rests on the validity of its predictions, i.e., is essentially an empirical question.

2. For simplicity, client firms are assumed to be all equity firms. The justification for modeling audit quality as the change in the client's share price is provided in Chapters 2 and 3, where we argue that audit services possess significant private good aspects. Watts and Zimmerman [1979] also model the ex ante benefits of an audit as incorporated in the client's share price.

3. See Appendix C for this and other requirements for membership in the SEC practice section of the American Institute of Certified Public Accountants.

4. In reality, with positive costs of changing auditors and learning-by-doing advantages, not all clients of an auditor who is caught "cheating" are likely to terminate the auditor. The tradeoff which these other clients face (the negative impact on firm value of retaining the auditor versus the costs of switching auditors) has changed, and thus the other clients are more likely to change auditors. Allowing the outcome to be probabilistic complicates the analysis without changing the qualitative predictions of the model.

5. The client's choice of a one period ($T=1$) or a two period ($T=2$) relationship with an auditor is simultaneously determined with the auditor's choice. The client's choice problem is formulated in Section 5.3.

6. This formulation implicitly assumes that the costs of coordinating $T=1$ time horizon clients are zero.

7. Only two period horizon ($T=2$) clients can serve as a collateral bond against auditor opportunism. This is the case because auditors earn zero profits on all one period ($T=1$) cleints, both at time zero and at time one. Auditors are indifferent between retaining and losing clients on which they earn zero economic profits. This, of course, presumes the absence of quality-guaranteeing or other sunk costs upon which auditors earn a future return.

8. In addition, n is a function of the parameters, r, w, and A_0, but we omit these parameters from the functional notation because we are not presently interested in predictions about changes in them.

9. The reasons why these particular rules were chosen are enumerated in Chapter 4. Also, see Appendix C for a detailed analysis of regulation requiring disclosure of auditor changes.

10. Notice that if $\phi_C(n^*) = 0$, the auditor's expected benefits from "cheating" will exceed those from not "cheating." One function of professional organizations like the AICPA may be to curtail auditor opportunism by raising $\phi_C(n^*)$. Measures such as mandatory peer review or mandatory audit committees composed of outside directors, for example, may serve this function. While it may not be in one individual auditor's narrow self interest to raise $\phi_C(n^*)$, it may be in the collective interest of auditors to do so. Thus, institutional arrangements (or regulation) may be an efficient means of accomplishing this goal.

11. While this formulation does not incorporate the moral or "psychic" costs to the auditor of "cheating," we are not implying that such costs may not be present—only that they are difficult to observe and quantify.

12. Only current $T=2$ clients can serve this quality-guaranteeing function in a two period model. Because they earn zero economic profits on new clients at time one, auditors will be indifferent between keeping and losing their clients. But see the caveat in footnote 1, this chapter.

13. This analysis assumes that only one client experiences financial difficulty such that the auditor has direct economic incentives to attest falsely. The analysis would become con-

Notes for Chapter 6

siderably more complex if the auditor had the incentive to "cheat" simultaneously on several clients. However, the result that increasing n^* lowers the probability of misrepresentation would still hold.

14. For simplicity, clients are assumed to be all-equity firms. In Chapters 2 and 3, we argued that auditing possesses significant private good aspects. This argument provides justification for modeling the total benefits from auditing as captured in the client's share price. See also Watts and Zimmerman [1979] for another model in which the ex ante benefits of the audit are incorporated in the client's share price.

15. As in the Chapter 4 "low-balling" model, we abstract from last period problems by assuming that all time one contracts are costlessly enforced.

16. The Envelope Theorem says that, for optimal values of the choice variables, the rate of change of the objective function with respect to a parameter, letting all the primary variables adjust, is equal to the rate of change letting no variables adjust. See Silberberg [1978, p. 168] for a proof of the Envelope Theorem for unconstrained maxima.

17. Observed auditor change rates are those of the firm's principal auditor. Firms may also have secondary auditors. Extant research into auditor change rates ignores secondary auditors. Their existence, however, poses interesting brand name questions, since secondary auditors are generally unnamed in the audit opinion.

Chapter 6

1. Again, what we mean by "industry" is a particular group of firms which exhibit significant differences from other groups, and significant similarities within the group. Such a group may be firms within a certain geographical area, within a certain industry, firms with a particular tax status (e.g., not-for-profit), or firms with a particular organizational form (e.g., professional partnerships).

2. The "Big Eight" public accounting firms are Arthur Andersen & Co., Arthur Young & Co., Coopers & Lybrand, Deloitte, Haskins & Sells, Ernst & Whinney, Peat, Marwick, Mitchell & Co., Price Waterhouse & Co., and Touche Ross & Co.

3. The cost function $c^i(l)$ may incorporate confidentiality or other industry costs not present in the cost function $c^i(n)$.

4. In this model, industry and firm-specific knowledge are acquired at time $t=0$ to be used at time $t=1$. This effect is analogous to the "volume effect" discussed in Alchian and Allen [1977] (pp. 260-62).

5. The optimal values are also functions of A_0, w, and r, but we are not currently interested in predictions about these parameters, so they are omitted from the functional notation.

6. A more realistic formulation would be to treat fee_0 and fee_0^I (and ϕ_R and ϕ_R^I) as functions of both n^* and l^*. However, the mathematical complexity introduced in this formulation obscures the intuition, while the comparative statics predictions are unchanged.

7. Because the decision problem is separable into two subdecisions,

$$\pi^i_{ln} = \pi^i_{nl} = 0.$$

Therefore, if the conditions $\pi^i_{nn} < 0$, $\pi^i_{ll} < 0$ are assumed to be satisfied, then the additional second order condition that

$$\pi^i_{nn} \pi^i_{ll} > (\pi^i_{nl})^2$$

is satisfied as well.

8. This is particularly a problem because of the length of the time period studied, i.e., 23 years.

Bibliography

Alchian, Armen A., "Why Money?" *Selected Works by Armen A. Alchian: Economic Forces at Work* (Indianapolis: Liberty Press, 1977).
_____, and Allen, William, *University Economics* (Belmont, California: Wadsworth Publishing Co., Inc., 1972).
_____, and Demsetz, Harold, "Production, Information Costs, and Economic Organization," *American Economic Review* (December 1972): 777-95.
American Institute of Certified Public Accountants, *Sample Engagement Letters for an Accounting Practice* (New York: AICPA, 1978).
Arens, A., and Loebbecke, James, *Auditing: An Integrated Approach* (Englewood Cliffs, New Jersey: Prentice-Hall, Inc., 1976).
Arnett, Harold, and Danos, Paul, *CPA Firm Viability* (Ann Arbor, Michigan: The University of Michigan, 1979).
Barefield, Russell M., and Beck, Paul J., "Competitive Bidding for Audit Engagements: A Framework for Analysis," Unpublished manuscript, University of Arizona (April 1979).
Barlev, Benzion, and Benston, George J., "Change of Auditors: An Analysis of the SEC's Reporting Requirement," Unpublished manuscript (1974).
Barzel, Yoram, "Measurement Cost and the Organization of Markets," Unpublished manuscript, University of Washington (July 1979).
_____, "Some Fallacies in the Interpretation of Information Costs," *Journal of Law and Economics* (October 1977): 291-307.
Bedingfield, James, "The Effect of Recent Litigation on Audit Practice," *Journal of Accountancy* (May 1974): 55-62.
Benston, George J., "Accounting Standards in the U.S. and the U.K.: Their Nature, Causes, and Consequences," *Vanderbilt Law Review* (January 1975): 235-68.
_____, "The Effectiveness and Effects of the SEC's Accounting Disclosure Requirements," in Henry G. Manne, ed., *Economic Policy and the Regulation of Corporate Securities* (Washington, D.C.: The American Enterprise Institute, 1969): 23-79.
_____, "The Market for Public Accounting Services: Demand, Supply, and Regulation," Unpublished Manuscript, University of Rochester (July 1979).
_____, "The Value of the SEC's Accounting Disclosure Requirements," *Accounting Review* (July 1969): 515-532.
Bolten, Steven E., and Crokett, John H., Jr., "How Independent Are the Independent Auditors?" *Financial Analysts' Journal* (November-December 1979): 76-78.
Burton, John C., and Roberts, William, "A Study of Auditor Changes," *Journal of Accountancy* (April 1967): 31-6.
Carpenter, Charles G., and Strawser, Robert H., "Displacement of Auditors when Clients Go Public," *Journal of Accountancy* (June 1971): 55-8.

Bibliography

Coe, Teddy L., and Palmon, Dan, "Some Evidence of the Magnitude of Auditor Turnover," Unpublished manuscript, New York University (October 1979).

Commission on Auditors' Responsibilities, *Report, Conclusions and Recommendations* (New York: Commission on Auditors' Responsibilities, 1978).

CPA Letter, "Why Companies Disagree with Their Auditors" (October 15, 1979).

Darby, Michael, and Karni, Edi, "Free Competition and the Optimal Amount of Fraud," *Journal of Law and Economics* (April 1973): 67-88.

DeAngelo, Linda, "Auditor Independence, 'Low Balling,' and Disclosure Regulation," *Journal of Accounting and Economics* (August 1981).

_____, "Auditor Size and Audit Quality," *Journal of Accounting and Economics* (December 1981).

Demsetz, Harold, "The Private Production of Public Goods," *Journal of Law and Economics* (October 1970): 293-306.

Dopuch, Nicholas, and Simunic, Dan, "The Nature of Competition in the Auditing Profession: A Descriptive and Normative View," paper presented at conference on Regulation and the Accounting Profession: An Exploration of the Issues, UCLA, May 24-25, 1979.

Edwards, James Don, *History of Public Accounting in the United States* (East Lansing, Michigan: Michigan State University, 1960).

Fama, Eugene, "Agency Problems and the Theory of the Firm," *Journal of Political Economy* (April 1980): 288-307.

_____, and Miller, Merton, *The Theory of Finance* (New York: Holt, Rinehart and Winston, 1972).

Financial Executives' Institute, "The Annual Audit Revisited," *Financial Executive* (March 1978): 38-44.

Fried, Dov, and Schiff, Allen, "CPA Switches and Associated Market Reactions," Working paper 79-8, The Vincent C. Ross Institute of Accounting Research, New York University (November 1979).

Guy, Dan, and Winters, Alan, "Unaudited Financial Statements: A Survey," *Journal of Accountancy* (December 1972): 46-53.

Hobgood, George, and Sciarrino, Joesph A., "Management Looks at Audit Services," *Financial Executive* (April 1972): 26-32.

_____, "Management Looks at Audit Services (Part II)," *Financial Executive* (August 1972): 24-5.

Jensen, Michael, and Meckling, William, "Theory of the Firm: Managerial Behavior, Agency Costs, and Capital Structure," *Journal of Financial Economics* (October 1976): 305-60.

Kaplan, Robert, "Supply and Demand for Auditing Services and the Nature of Regulations in Auditing: A Critique," *Arthur Young Professors' Roundtable Conference Proceedings* (1978): 125-31.

Klein, Benjamin, Crawford, Robert, and Alchian, Armen, "Vertical Integration, Appropriable Rents and the Competitive Contracting Process," *Journal of Law and Economics* (October 1978): 297-321.

_____, and Leffler, Keith, "The Role of Price in Guaranteeing Quality," forthcoming, *Journal of Political Economy.*

Macaulay, Stewart, "Non-Contractual Relations in Business: A Preliminary Study," *American Sociological Review* (1963): 55-67.

Magee, Robert, "Regulation and the Cost-Effectiveness of Independent Audits by CPA,'s" Unpublished manuscript, Northwestern Universtiy (April 1979).

Mayers, David, and Smith, Clifford, "Toward A Positive Theory of Insurance," Unpublished manuscript, University of Rochester (August 1979).

Ng, David, "Supply and Demand of Auditing Services and the Nature of Regulations in Auditing," *Arthur Young Professors' Roundtable Conference Proceedings* (1978): 99-124.

Rhode, John Grant, Witsell, Gary M., and Kelsey, Richard L., "An Analysis of Client-Industry Concentrations for Large Public Accounting Firms," *Accounting Review* (October 1974): 772-87.

Ronen, Joshua, "The Dual Role of Accounting: A Financial Economic Perspective," in James L. Bicksler, ed., *Handbook of Financial Economics* (Amsterdam: North-Holland Publishing Co., 1979): 415-454.

Schiff, Allen, and Fried, H. Dov, "Large Companies and the Big Eight: An Overview," *Abacus* (1976): 116-24.

Securities and Exchange Commission, *Accounting Series Release No. 250* (June 1976).

_____, *Securities Act of 1933, Release No. 5869* (September 1977).

_____, *Securities Exchange Act of 1934, Release No. 9344* (September 1971).

Silberberg, Eugene, *The Structure of Economics: A Mathematical Analysis* (New York: McGraw-Hill, 1978).

Smith, Clifford and Warner, Jerold, "On Financial Contracting: An Analysis of Bond Covenants," *Journal of Financial Economics* (June 1979): 117-161.

Staff Study, *The Accounting Establishment,* prepared by the Subcommittee on Reports, Accounting and Management of the Committee on Governmental Affairs, United States Senate, (Washington, D.C.: U.S. Government Printing Office, 1976).

Wallace, Wanda, "Discussant's Comments: Some Consideration on Auditor Turnover" (August 1979), mimeograph.

Watts, Ross L., "Corporate Financial Statements, A Product of the Market and Political Processes," *Australian Journal of Management* (April 1977): 53-75.

_____, and Milne, Frank, "Corporate Information: A Private or Public Good?" Unpublished manuscript, University of Rochester (August 1977).

_____, and Zimmerman, Jerold L., "Auditors and the Determination of Accounting Standards," Working paper No. GPB 78-06, University of Rochester (March 1979).

_____, "The Market for Independence and Independent Auditors," Unpublished manuscript, University of Rochester (July 1979).

_____, "Towards A Positive Theory of the Determination of Accounting Standards," *Accounting Review* (January 1978): 112-34.

Williamson, Oliver, *Markets and Hierarchies: Analysis and Antitrust Implications* (New York: Free Press, 1975).

Willingham, John, and Carmichael, D.R., *Auditing Concepts and Methods* (New York: McGraw-Hill, 1975).

Yocum, James, *Public Accounting Firm Practices and CPA Attitudes in Ohio* (Columbus, Ohio: Center for Business and Economic Research, The Ohio State University, 1972).

Zeff, Stephen A., and Fossum, Robert L., "An Analysis of Large Audit Clients," *Accounting Review* (April 1967): 298-320.

References for Appendix D

American Institute of Certified Public Accountants, *Sample Engagement Letters for an Accounting Practice* (New York, AICPA, 1978).

Bedingfield, James, "The Effect of Recent Litigation on Audit Practice," *Journal of Accountancy* (May 1974): 55-62.

Guy, Dan, and Winters, Alan, "Unaudited Financial Statements: A Survey," *Journal of Accountancy* (December 1972): 46-53.

Yocum, James, *Public Accounting Firm Practices and CPA Attitudes in Ohio* (Columbus, Ohio: Center for Business and Economic Research, The Ohio State University, 1972).

Index

Advertising, 30
  professional ban on, 96
Agency costs, 9-10
  definition of, 7-8
AICPA, 25-26, 28, 34, 38-39, 48, 79, 120
AICPA Council, 25
Alchian, Armen, 1, 55, 113, 115, 117-18, 121
Allen, William, 115, 121
Arens, A., 35, 79
Arnett, Harold, 79, 81
Arthur Andersen & Co., 92, 121
Arthur Young & Co., 121
ASR-165 on auditor changes, 46-47, 49, 62, 73-75, 97
ASR-194 on auditor changes, 46
ASR-247 on auditor changes, 46
ASR-250 on auditor-client relationships, 2-3, 39, 48, 97
Assumptions, role of, in theory, 19, 56, 95, 119
Audit fee limitations, 2. *See also* ASR-250 on auditor-client relationships
Audit firms
  "Big Eight," 24, 72, 80, 93, 117, 121
  discipline of, 25-26
  size of, 65
  structured as continuing partnerships, 25, 28
Auditing
  as minimum cost monitoring arrangement, 10, 14-16
  positive theory of, 1-2, 10
  as a sorting mechanism, 12-13
Auditor brand name. *See* Brand name, auditor
Auditor changes
  empirical evidence about, 72-76
  predictions about, 72-76
  regulation governing, 46-47, 120
Auditor concentration
  definition of, 62
  predictions about, 62-63, 72
Auditor independence
  definitions of, 34
  regulatory concern, 2, 34, 46-47
  See also "Low balling", and auditor independence
Auditor input, 17
  as a surrogate for auditor output, 24, 117
Auditor rotation, mandatory. *See* Mandatory auditor rotation
Audit output, 17, 22-23, 40
  observability of, 5, 22-24
Audit procedures, 17
Audit process, 18, 33, 40
Audit quality
  costs of evaluating, 24-25
  definition of, 17, 23, 40, 59, 116, 119
  direct observation of, 116
  incentives to specialize in uniform, 24

Barefield, Russell M., 18, 22, 113
Bargaining power. *See* Relative bargaining power
Barlev, Benzion, 113
Barzel, Yoram, 13, 22, 24, 31, 114, 117
Beck, Paul J., 18, 22, 113
Benston, George J., 7, 10, 26, 28-29, 113-14
"Big Eight" audit firms. *See* Audit firms, "Big Eight"
Bilateral monopoly, 37, 41, 43, 47, 53, 119. *See also* "Small numbers bargaining situation"
Bolton, Steven E., 113
Bond
  collateral, use of explicit, 27, 117-18
  covenants, 12
Bondholder expropriation strategies, 11-12, 15, 114
Bonding expenditures, definition of, 8
Brand name
  auditor, 5-6, 18, 23-24, 27-29, 116, 119
  in general, 24, 29-32
Burton, John C., 113

Carmichael, D. R., 17

Index

Carpenter, Charles G., 113
Certified Public Accountants, 10, 25
  discipline of, 25
Client relationships, 30
Coe, Teddy L., 73-74, 93-94, 113
Cohen Commission. *See* Commission on Auditors' Responsibilities
Cohen Report. *See* Report of the Commission on Auditors' Responsibilities
Collateral bond. *See* Bond, collateral, use of explicit
Commission on Auditors' Responsibilities, 2, 38, 46-49, 55, 65, 80
Confidentiality costs, definition of, 81-82
Contracting costs, differential, 26
Contracts
  explicit vs. implicit, 53-54
  long term vs. short term, 53
Coopers & Lybrand, 92, 121
Coordination costs, definition of, 57
Costs. *See* Confidentiality costs; Contracting costs; Coordination costs; Search costs; Start-up costs
Costless contracting, 26, 42, 118
Crawford, Robert, 55, 117-18
Credence goods, 29, 116
Crockett, John H., Jr., 113

Danos, Paul, 79, 81
Darby, Michael, 29-31, 117
DeAngelo, Linda, 113, 116
Deloitte, Haskins & Sells, 92, 121
Demsetz, Harold, 113, 115-17
Disclosure regulation, 10, 12-14
Dopuch, Nicholas, 18, 22, 28, 93-94, 113

"Economic interest" concept, definition of, 3, 34
Edwards, James Don, 117
Engagement letters, 52
Envelope theorem, 71-72, 121
Ernst & Ernst. *See* Ernst & Whinney
Ernst & Whinney, 31, 92, 121
Ex post "settling up", 27-28

Fama, Eugene, 9, 28, 113-14
FASB-12 on marketable equity securities, 79
FASB-19 on petroleum accounting, 79
Financial Executives' Institute, 74-75
Firm, theory of the, 1
Fossum, Robert L., 5, 91-93, 113
Fraud, definition of, 29-30
Free rider problem, 5, 17-20, 115
  intrashareholder, 18-20
  See also Public goods problem
Fried, Dov, 92-93, 113

GAAP, 55
GAAS, 25, 55, 118

Haskins & Sells. *See* Deloitte, Haskins & Sells
Hobgood, George, 53

Industry
  diversification by auditors, 81
  learning-by-doing advantages, 4, 78-79, 121
  specialization by auditors, 4, 80-81, 91-94
Information assymetry
  between auditors and consumers of audit services, 24
  between current and potential owners, 10-11, 21-22
  between owners and managers, 9
  between producers and consumers, 32

Jensen, Michael, 7-8, 10, 113-14
Joint ownership, as a response to free rider problems, 20-22

Kaplan, Robert, 22, 113
Karni, Edi, 29-31, 116
Kelsey, Richard L., 92-93, 113
Klein, Benjamin, 31-32, 55, 117-18

"Last period" problems, 27-28, 36, 118
Learning-by-doing advantages, 35, 41
  industry. *See* Industry, learning-by-doing advantages
Leffler, Keith, 31-32, 118
Length of the auditor-client relationship, 6, 55, 67-76
  See also Auditor changes
Loebbecke, James, 35, 79
"Low balling"
  and auditor independence, 37-39, 49
  definition of, 2, 46
  and disclosure regulation, 46-49, 113
  regulatory concern, 2, 39, 47-49
Lybrand, Ross Bros. & Montgomery. *See* Coopers & Lybrand

Macaulay, Stewart, 53-54
Magee, Robert, 18, 22, 113
Mandatory auditor rotation, 38, 55-56. *See also* Auditor changes, regulation governing; ASR-165 on auditor changes
Mayers, David, 117
Meckling, William, 7-8, 10, 113-14
Metcalf Subcommittee. *See* Subcommittee on Reports, Accounts and Management
Miller, Merton, 114
Milne, Frank, 19
Monitoring expenditures, definition of, 8

Index

Monopoly, bilateral. *See* Bilateral monopoly; "Small numbers bargaining situation"

National Association of Certified Public Accountants, 117
Ng, David, 18-20, 22-23, 113, 116

Opportunistic behavior, definition of, 53, 113
"Oversearching", 12

Palmon, Dan, 73-74, 93-94, 113
Peat Marwick, Mitchell & Co., 31, 92, 121
Peat, Marwick, Mitchell Foundation, 31
Positive theory of auditing. *See* Auditing, positive theory of
"Price protection", 11, 16
Price, "quality guaranteeing". *See* "Quality guaranteeing price"
Price Waterhouse & Co., 92, 121
Private Practice Section of AICPA, 25-26
Proportional sharing rule, 20, 22
Public good
 assertion in auditing, 5, 18-22
 problem, 19, 115
 See also Free rider problem
Public Oversight Board, 25

"Quality guaranteeing price", 31-32, 116-17

Regulation. *See* Disclosure regulation
Relative bargaining power, 41-42, 63, 118
Repeat sales mechanism, 27
Report of the Commission on Auditors' Responsibilities, 26, 38-39, 46-48, 80, 116
Residual loss, definition of, 8
"Reverse cheating", 27
Rhode, John Grant, 92-93, 113
Roberts, William, 113
Ronen, Joshua, 114

Schiff, Allen, 92-93, 113
Sciarrino, Joseph A., 53

Search costs, 12-13, 24
SEC, 2-3, 25-26, 34, 38-39, 46-47, 73, 117
SEC Practice Section of AICPA, 25, 56, 120
Securities Act Release No. 33-5869, 2, 39
Securities Exchange Act Release No. 34-9344, 46-47, 62, 73, 75
Shareholders as auditors, 114
Silberberg, Eugene, 121
Simunic, Dan, 18, 22, 28, 93-94, 113
"Small numbers bargaining situation", 36-37
 See also Bilateral monopoly
Smith, Clifford, 12, 114, 117
Specialized assets
 and auditor independence, 36
 definition of, 35, 41
 and "low-balling", 38
 non-marketability of, 37
Start-up costs, 35
Strawser, Robert H., 113
Subcommittee on Reports, Accounts and Management, 55, 65, 80, 98

Touche, Ross & Co., 92, 121
Touche, Ross, Bailey & Smart. *See* Touche, Ross & Co.

Uniform CPA Exam, 25

Vertical integration of auditors, 54-55

Wallace, Wanda, 74, 113
Warner, Jerold, 12, 114
Watts, Ross, 1-2, 7, 19, 26, 28, 113-14, 116, 119, 121
Whitsell, Gary M., 92-93, 113
Williamson, Oliver, 36, 53
Willingham, John, 17
Working papers, 17, 118

Zeff, Stephen A., 4, 91-93, 113
Zimmerman, Jerold L., 1, 7, 26, 28, 113-14, 116, 119, 121